Endorsements for *The Mulligan*

"For those who have learned that golf is more than just a game, *The Mulligan* will be welcome reading that will provide helpful insights not just for their golf game, but for their lives as well."

> —Ben Crenshaw, two time Masters Champion and
> 2002 inductee to the World Golf Hall of Fame

"Wally Armstrong and Ken Blanchard not only understand golf but life and the value of relationships. They have put together a story that should warm your heart, help your golf game, and just may touch your life."

> —Jack Nicklaus, golf legend and 1974 inductee
> to the World Golf Hall of Fame

"I really enjoyed reading *The Mulligan* and I know my dad, Harvey, would have loved this simple little book because there are so many things in it that embody the wisdom, grace, and the importance of friendships my dad always treasured."

> —Tinsley Penick, PGA golf professional

"A compelling story about the importance of a mulligan. It may only happen on the first tee in golf, but in the game of life it is there for the asking, provided you are prepared to ask and know the One who has the answer."

> —C. William Pollard, Chairman of The ServiceMaster
> Company and author of *The Soul of the Firm*

"If you want to improve your golf game and your life, reading *The Mulligan* is a must. It's a spiritual journey down the fairway."

> —John C. Maxwell, author, speaker, and founder
> of INJOY Stewardship and EQUIP

"Every now and then we need a wake-up call to remind us of the things in life that really matter. Thankfully, Wally Armstrong and Ken Blanchard in their book, *The Mulligan*, reassure us that second chances to correct our wrongs are just one swing away!"

—Paul J. Meyer, New York Times best-selling author
and founder of Success Motivation International, Inc.

In *The Mulligan*, Wally Armstrong and Ken Blanchard strike a common chord among sportsmen and those seeking a better understanding of the broader arena which is life itself. The lessons of second chances, forgiveness, and love are eternal as espoused by the great "Old Pro" himself: Jesus Christ."

—Pete McDaniel, best-selling author and
Senior Writer for *Golf Digest*

"As we walk the fairways of life, this great game teaches us early on that if we continue in our dedication to perfection good things may happen. The same holds true in our own lives; dedication, hard work, and trial and error will be rewarded. *The Mulligan* sets the stage for that perfect score. Great job Wally & Ken!"

—Jerry Rich, owner Rich Harvest Farms,
site of the 2009 Solheim Cup

"If golf is a metaphor for life, then a mulligan is a perfect metaphor for God's love. Ken Blanchard's new book is a terrific reminder that whenever we ask, God gives us second chances throughout our lives and straight on into eternity."

—Bill Jones III, chairman and CEO of Sea Island Company

"*The Mulligan* helped my attitude toward golf, life and God and this is rarely accomplished in one book. It's really a great book!"

—Lou Holtz, former head coach , NCAA football

The Mulligan

EVERYONE NEEDS A SECOND CHANCE
IN GOLF AND IN LIFE

by WALLY ARMSTRONG
and KEN BLANCHARD

Published by
THOMAS NELSON
Since 1798
www.thomasnelson.com

Published in Nashville, Tennessee by Thomas Nelson, Inc.

Thomas Nelson, Inc. titles may be purchased in bulk for educational, business, fundraising, or sales promotional use. For information, please email SpecialMarkets@ThomasNelson.com.

All Scripture quotations, unless otherwise indicated, are taken from The Holy Bible, New International Version (NIV). Copyright © 1973, 1978, 1984. International Bible Society. Used by permission of Zondervan Bible Publishers.

Editorial Staff: David Moberg, acquisitions editor; Thom Chittom, managing editor
Page Design: Lori Lynch, Book & Graphic Design, Nashville, TN
Cover Design: Chris Tobias

Library of Congress Cataloging-in-Publication Data

Armstrong, Wally.
  The Mulligan : everyone needs a second chance in golf and in life / by Wally Armstrong and Ken Blanchard.
     p. cm.
  Includes bibliographical references and index.
  ISBN 10: 0-8499-0323-8
  ISBN 13: 978-0-8499-0323-6
  1. Golfers—Religious life. 2. Golf—Religious aspects—Christianity.
3. Christian life. I. Blanchard, Kenneth H. II. Title.

BV4596.G64A77 2006
248.4—dc22   2006100416

Printed in the United States of America
07 08 09 10 11 QW 5 4 3

Contents

"*MULLIGAN*," in golf (n)—In friendly play, permission granted a golfer by the other players to retake a flubbed shot especially the first shot of the game. Golf's generous forgiveness, The Mulligan, originated in the U.S. at Winged Foot Golf Club created via David B. Mulligan. This second chance shot is not allowed by the official rules of golf.

This Book
is Dedicated to
Duke Dupree
Harvey Penick
Davis Love, Jr.
and
All the Old Pros
Who Teach Us
about
Golf and Life

Foreword

*A*s a young lad, my passion for golf grew out of the cornfields of Indiana. I hawked golf balls in the fields lining the local nine-hole Indian Lake Country Club. On a good day, my pockets were full of balls to be sold for a few nickels and dimes. But the real money came through caddying and shagging balls for the club champion Duke Dupree.

Duke saw my love and desire to play, so he taught me the disciplines of the game. More than that, he helped me to believe in myself. He saw all the dormant possibilities in my life and made me believe they could come true. Duke was more than an employer. He was a teacher, brother, friend, and a father in many ways; Duke's impact on my life is immeasurable. Many times during my 300-plus PGA Tour events, I have sensed Duke standing there beside me, encouraging me in the execution of the shot at hand.

Besides the wisdom of Duke Dupree, this book reflects the influence of two other men. One of these is the legendary golf professional Harvey Penick, author of *Harvey Penick's Little Red Book* (Simon & Schuster, 1992). It is no accident that one of *The Mulligan's* main characters, Old Pro Willie Dunn, resembles Harvey in many ways. Harvey always thought of himself as a grown-up caddy, and many of us share the same opinion. Caddies used to be found at every golf facility from the muni's to the country clubs. Being a caddy provided thousands of young men and women an opportunity to get bit by the golf bug. Davis Love Jr., a renowned golf instructor who was tragically killed in a plane crash, is another key influence, and his son, PGA Tour player Davis Love III, is a key character in the book. Harvey Penick was the golf coach at the University of Texas when Davis Love Jr. was a player there. Shortly after leaving the PGA tour full-time in 1985, I had the privilege of observing Davis Jr. teach golf. What a thrill that was! He had a gentle yet firm, loving way of teaching through homespun language and analogies. All three of these men—Duke, Harvey, and Davis—

guided me in the development of the characters and story-line for this book. Their approach to life and golf fits its message to a tee.

One thing Duke taught me is that life is all about relationships, which you will hear from the Old Pro on the following pages. Our hearts are designed for meaningful friendships which are treasures of great value. Deep relationships should go with us all along the course of our lives. I have been truly blessed with friends. Ken Blanchard is one great friend.

When I met Ken a few years ago we connected instantly because we love the game and understand the great value of relationships. We believe that through relationships and second chances in life we have both gained a stronger grip on who we are and what is our ultimate purpose for living. That is why our message is that life is a bowl full of mulligans—second chances abound! Every one of us needs to take and learn from them. And, as we do, we will be strengthened to play the course laid out before us in golf and in life.

It is our sincere desire that this little book will bring joy and hope your way.

—*Wally Armstrong*
July 2006

1

The Executive

"Late as usual," Paul McAllister mumbled to himself in a frustrated tone. Being late for his tee-off time for the Pro-Am at the Biltmore Forest Country Club in Asheville, North Carolina, was the last thing he wanted to happen. Playing in this Pro-Am was something he had wanted to do for a long time, and especially after last night. He had flown in yesterday afternoon from Atlanta for the Pro-Am Pairing Party. Paul was ecstatic when his foursome had drawn Davis Love III, because Love, year after year, was one of the greatest players on the PGA golf tour. His father, Davis Love Jr., had been considered one of the best teachers of the game anywhere.

What an opportunity, thought McAllister. *Maybe Love can help me with my golf game.*

Paul's attitude toward golf was the same attitude he had toward everything: he wanted to be the best. At forty-five, life to him was still one achievement game after another. He had gone to an Ivy League school, working hard to make sure he ranked near the top of his class. He was president or captain of everything he joined. Paul was driven. Everything for him was about getting ahead—get into a good graduate school; land a job with the best possible company; stay one step in front of the next guy—and he was very successful.

The only failure Paul ever had was his marriage. Right after he earned his MBA, he married Rebecca, his college sweetheart. She was one of the most popular girls on campus. Everybody wanted her, but he beat out the competition. He secretly enjoyed the fact that if he had fumbled his lines at the wedding ceremony at least three in his wedding party would have stepped forward to take his place. Once the wedding ceremony was over, Paul figured that the marriage job was done. Now he could get back to work.

After five years of trying to find some way of being part of Paul's life, including having a son, Rebecca filed for divorce. She tried everything—even suggesting marriage counseling—but Paul never had time. It wasn't important to him. He was too busy being an entrepreneur and building his business. After working for a great company for two years he had decided to go out on his own. He worked harder than ever. But there were consequences. Just as Paul had predicted, the marriage job was done. His wife and child were out of his life. And though there was some initial pain and regret, Paul took it as a career-enhancing change.

Free to focus on the business he started three years before, Paul grew it into a multi-million dollar operation. When McAllister looked at his life, he thought that real success had to do with the amount of wealth he accumulated, the amount of recognition he got for his efforts and the power and status he achieved. But after fifteen years of experiencing the momentary highs from making one hot deal after another, Paul still felt something was missing. It was not enough.

Even though people who grew up with Paul—like the classmates he saw at a recent twenty-fifth high school reunion—viewed him as very successful, that did not comfort him. No matter what he achieved, it never was enough. The job was never done. Instead of slowing down to find out why, Paul was always looking for the next mountain to climb. And for Paul, that next mountain was golf.

Golf became the second singular passion in Paul's life. Golf was the one connection he shared with his functioning alcoholic father. Paul's happiest memories were of late summer afternoons spent with his dad walking the public course near their home. His dad took off work early to teach him the game. But when his dad died in a car accident; that shining period was over. His dad's death left the twelve-year-old Paul feeling abandoned and alone. Now a grown man, Paul's life was an unending mission to fill the void.

2

A Trauma

As he approached the clubhouse at the golf course Paul was a little annoyed—no one was waiting to take his bag. When a youngster finally showed up, Paul was short with him. Giving the kid his bag, Paul hurried off to the registration desk without giving him a tip. After registering, he realized that he had only thirty minutes until his tee-off time. *Not much time to warm up,* Paul thought. He headed quickly to the driving range to beat as many balls as possible before he had to go to the first tee.

Waiting for him at the tee were three other amateurs. Paul had met them at the Pairing Party the night before. But after finding out what they did for a living and who they didn't know, he had written off the group as not important enough for him to get to know. As a result, he shook their hands in a cursory way. His main concern was the whereabouts of their pro member, Davis Love III.

Just as the starter asked if the eleven-thirty group was ready to go, Love walked through the crowd and onto the tee. He had a warm smile on his face as he introduced himself to each of his amateur playing partners.

As Paul shook Davis's hand he was wondering how he could make Love realize that *he* was the most important member of the group. Paul had taken a number of lessons during the last three weeks in preparation for this tournament. Maybe his golf game would pave the way to a relationship with Love.

Affecting graciousness, Paul encouraged his three playing partners to hit first after Love sent a towering drive from the back tee down the middle of the fairway well over three hundred yards away. As Paul watched each of his playing partners hit their drives, a small grin appeared on his face. He realized these guys were real hackers—twenty handicappers at best. And here he was, a twelve handicap who should soon be a single digit player.

When it came Paul's turn to hit he walked confidently to the tee box, teed up his ball, and stepped back to look up the fairway toward the hole. His caddy broke in, "The best spot to hit your drive on this hole is the right center of the fairway. It opens up the hole from there, especially given where they've set the pin today." The caddie's advice broke Paul's concentration. *I hope he is not going to talk in my ear all day*, thought Paul. *I know how to play this game.*

With that he stepped up to the ball, swung too hard, and hit a wild hook. Not only did it not end up on the right side of the fairway, but it landed in heavy rough on the left. He glanced quickly around the gallery to see if there was anybody taking any pictures that he could blame. He'd seen top pros do this many times on TV. But when he looked in Davis's direction, the pro wasn't paying attention. He didn't even care where Paul's shot had gone. (Later, Paul learned that Davis Love knew the secret of playing in Pro-Ams: don't watch the amateurs swing. Play your own game. You don't want a lot of negative images filling your mind, particularly if that is how you make your living.)

Paul's hook off the first tee was a sign of things to come. He went from bad to worse. While his higher-handicap playing partners were short off the tee, they were straight and kept on bogeying holes. Paul, on the other hand, hit his tee shots long but they were wild. He ended up contributing double bogeys. He picked up on more holes than he finished. Paul did everything he could to fix his swing, but nothing seemed to work. As they reached the ninth hole, Paul really was losing it: he wasn't developing relationships with Love or his playing partners and he wasn't having fun.

Paul's negative self-talk began to take over, as usual.

You idiot, he thought. *This is embarrassing! How can you play like this? Those lessons certainly didn't help.*

When it came his turn to tee off, Paul quieted his mind for the first time during the round and lo and behold he hit a perfect drive that brought a smile to his face. *Now I am going to get it together,* he thought. He followed his drive with a beautiful four iron that bounced on the center of the green and stopped four feet from the cup. Even the crowd gathered around the green waiting to see Davis Love applauded Paul as he approached.

After Davis and his playing partners had putted out, it was Paul's turn. Paul felt his blood pressure rise. Since this was the number-two-handicap hole on the card, he got a stroke. If he could make this birdie putt, it would mean an eagle for his team. Even Davis Love sensed that, and helped Paul read the putt. But when he stroked the ball it came up three inches short of the cup—the dreaded "never up, never in." Paul thought of Yogi Berra's line: "Ninety percent of the putts that are short don't go in."

Tapping the ball into the cup for par, Paul completely lost it. He took his putter and hurled it into a nearby lake. Everybody around him—including the caddies—slowly walked away in silence, leaving him alone on the green.

Paul didn't know whether to cry or yell. Realizing that he would have to putt the rest of the round with a two iron or a wood, Paul rolled up his pants and waded into the lake to retrieve his putter. What he had hoped would be a wonderful day had turned into a nightmare.

When Paul finally headed for the tenth tee Davis Love was waiting for him.

"Paul," he said in a caring voice, "we haven't talked much during the first nine holes, but I have been watching you. And to be honest, you aren't good enough to get that mad. What you just did on the ninth green may have as much to say about where you are with your life as your game. Think about it." With that, Love headed to the tee to hit his shot.

Love's comments froze Paul in his tracks. He was deeply embarrassed—probably for the first time in his life (at least that he would admit). He wondered if he should just quit and walk to his car. But Love's remarks had hooked him. They made him want to stay.

Walking down from the tenth tee, Paul waited for Love to catch up; Love hit his drive from the back tee, almost seventy-five yards further than where the amateurs hit. As Love walked up, Paul was almost too choked up to speak.

"What you said to me," Paul finally managed, "hit me like a ton of bricks. I apologize. I've been a real jerk."

3

The Mentor

s they continued to walk down the fairway, Love said, "That's okay, Paul. I have played in a lot of Pro-Ams. It's hard watching what people do to themselves on the golf course. I make a living playing golf and you make a living doing something else, but what we do on the golf course often reflects how we live our lives. My father always taught me that life and golf have a lot in common. In fact, Dad used to say that golf spells **G**ame **O**f **L**ife **F**irst."

Paul laughed for the first time during the round. "I always heard this game was called golf because all the other four-letter words were taken. But now that I think about it, I like your acronym better than my joke."

"So do I," said Davis with a smile. "If he were still alive, I would suggest you go see my father. Not only was he a great teacher of the game of golf, he was a great teacher of the game of life. But there is an old friend of his who I think could really help you. Everyone who knows him calls him the Old Pro. His name is Willie Dunn.

"The Old Pro," Love continued, "was named after his grandfather, Old Willie Dunn. He was a famous Scottish golf course designer and teacher in the mid-eighteen hundreds. His father John Duncan Dunn was a golf professional and came over to the United States in 1898 to teach and design golf courses in Florida and California. So with a family background like that, Willie won his share of trophies until his competitive playing career ended tragically from a shoulder wound during World War II. After the war, he settled in Asheville, North Carolina, and he's been teaching golf here for over sixty years.

"I think you'll find him on the porch by the clubhouse at the end of the round," Davis continued. "He loves to sit there and watch golfers come and go—watch life go by. Willie is almost ninety now, but he is as sharp as a tack and one of the wisest men I know. I recommend you spend some time with him. Tell him I sent you."

After talking to Davis, Paul was amazed how relaxed he felt over the back nine. And guess what? He played better. Even though Davis's words had been hard to hear, Paul realized he was right. Here he was, grinding his teeth over a game he didn't spend that much time perfecting. Yet he expected outstanding performance on every shot! He also thought about the relationship between golf and life and he realized he was feeling down about both right now.

Paul had always been a stickler for enforcing rules. So he never really liked the common practice of granting players a mulligan off the first tee, without penalty, if their initial drive was not to their liking. Despite the fact that Paul had been in situations where he could have offered a fellow player a mulligan or could have accepted one for himself, he did neither. His pride would never let him accept charity or give it. Nevertheless, he had really blown the chance of a lifetime today. He would have loved to play the front nine over again without any consequences. It would have been a whole different experience. He smiled to himself as he visualized a mulligan first nine. *That would be the ultimate mulligan*, he thought.

Paul laughed recalling his first visit to Scotland. It was there that he really learned that hitting a mulligan requires the goodwill of those with whom you are playing. The first course they played was Turnberry, where the British Open has been played several times. When Paul's playing partner hit his initial drive into the rough, he turned to the starter and asked, "Could I have a mulligan?" Without changing his expression the starter said, "If you take a mulligan in Scotland, you are shooting three."

At the end of the round, Paul shook hands with his team members and walked quietly over to Davis. Pointing up at the porch, Davis said, "The Old Pro's there. You can't miss him. He is sitting on the rocker to the far left."

"Thanks for your help and advice," Paul said.

"Good luck. I have a hunch the Old Pro will help you with more than just your golf game."

4

The Beginning of a
New Lease on Life

fter his caddy cleaned his clubs and sent them up to the parking lot to be placed in his car, Paul headed toward the clubhouse. As he approached, he saw the Old Pro sitting in the rocker. He was wearing knickers and argyle socks. The wrinkles on the back of his neck were deep and crisscrossed, like a roadmap that had been folded over and over again. Paul was struck by the warm smile on the man's face. He smiled back and said, "Davis Love said I ought to talk to you."

The Old Pro smiled. "Sit down, son," he said.

Taking a seat, Paul asked, "What should I call you, sir?"

"Just call me Will," said the old man. "My last name

is Dunn, so I like to think that maybe at the end of my life I will hear, 'Will Dunn!'" The Old Pro smiled.

Not understanding the gist of the Old Pro's humor, Paul responded, "Okay, Will, that sounds good to me."

"What did you do out there, son, that Davis sent you my way?"

"Well, sir, I think I was taking the game too seriously, just like I always do. I was trying to impress Love and my teammates with my ability, but hit an ugly shot off the first tee. Then things went from bad to worse. Finally, on the ninth hole, I hit a great drive and a beautiful second shot four feet from the cup—but I left the putt short. When that happened, I lost it and threw that ugly putter into the lake. Davis spoke to me privately after my blow up and really opened my eyes to what I was doing to myself."

"Enough said," responded the Old Pro with a sympathetic smile.

"What Davis told me hit me like a ton of bricks—it really impacted me. It cut me to the core. Do you have time so we can talk?" asked Paul.

The Old Pro said slowly in a caring way, "All the time in the world, son."

"Davis said that you could straighten out not only my golf game, but maybe my life as well."

"That's a tall order," said the Old Pro. "But golf and life do have a great deal in common. Golf has a way of showing what is going on inside someone. As Davis probably told you, his father and I agreed that to master the game of golf you have to master the **Game Of Life First.**"

"He did," said Paul. "Could you tell me more?"

"Sure," said the Old Pro with a smile. "In life, as in golf—

- You get good breaks you deserve
- You get good breaks you don't deserve
- You get bad breaks you deserve
- You get bad breaks you don't deserve
- Sometimes you are performing or playing better than you should and you have to deal with success
- Sometimes you are performing or playing worse than you should and you have to deal with failure.

"In golf this all takes place in four-and-a-half hours with that little ball staring at you and nobody there to hit it but yourself. In life it occurs every moment of every day."

"That's interesting," said Paul. "I never thought of it that way. Where would we start if you were to help me with my life and my golf game?"

"Son, *life is all about relationships*. We have to get to

know each other. That means we need to spend some time together. When are you going to get back this way?"

"As soon as possible," said Paul. "In fact, maybe I could stay over until tomorrow. What's your schedule?" Paul couldn't believe he'd said that. Relationships just weren't his thing. But the embarrassment he felt about chucking his putter in front of Davis Love III had been a significant emotional event—what some people might call "a cosmic goose." Paul thought that maybe getting close to the Old Pro would give him a chance to redeem himself with Love.

Responding to Paul's question, the Old Pro said, "At my age, son, I don't like to get up at the crack of dawn anymore. Why don't we meet at the Muni at ten o'clock tomorrow morning."

"What's the Muni?" asked Paul.

"That's the municipal course on the other side of town. It's not as fancy as this place but it works just fine. It's where I learned the game of golf and the game of life."

Shaking the Old Pro's hand, Paul said, "Thanks. See you tomorrow at ten."

5

Reflection

aul spent a thoughtful dinner by himself that night. Something about the Old Pro really got to him when he said "Life is all about relationships." Deep down inside, there was something waking up in Paul that had been buried long ago. But before he could figure out what it was, his skeptical side kicked in.

Is this man for real? Can I really trust him? thought Paul. He certainly could never count on his father. He never knew which father he was going to get. Would it be the one with whom he enjoyed playing golf or the abusive drunk who was critical of everything he did? Paul was always looking for that little ounce of praise. But it never came. His dad died when Paul needed him most.

Later in his teen years, Paul was drawn to the basketball coach at his school. The coach had befriended him, and had even taught him to play golf again. Paul idolized him; but he abandoned Paul. The coach left town with a fair-haired teacher with whom he'd been conducting a secret affair. There was no attempt to say goodbye.

After that, Paul decided he couldn't trust anybody but himself. It was best to go it alone in life. His drive to be a super achiever kicked into high gear. He became a "human doing" not a human being, looking to his performance for significance. Relationships became secondary, even, eventually, his relationship with his son Jake. Inside Paul was afraid: afraid of getting hurt again by investing too much in his relationships; afraid that if he let his guard down people would see things in him that even he didn't want to admit. That made him vulnerable.

But the Old Pro seemed different somehow. Maybe Paul's life really wasn't working as well as it should, and his golf game could use some help.

Later that night, as Paul got ready for bed, he committed to begin writing a journal. Maybe that would help him keep track of the ideas firing in his mind. For years people had told him that journaling was a good process, but he never wanted to do it. A Type A personality, if Paul was going to write a journal, he wanted to do it better

than anybody else. He knew people who did their jour-
nalizing in four colors. Others wrote poetry in their jour-
nals. How could he begin to compete with that?

Paul had recently read an article about journaling that
suggested a simple, non-competitive format. The idea was
that at the end of the day or early the next morning, you'd
write "Yesterday" at the top of a journal page and start off
by praising yourself for things you'd done well that day.
These were things that made you feel good about yourself
because they were consistent with what you had hoped to
accomplish or whom you wanted to be in the world. Paul
wasn't quite sure what to make of the latter reason. Whom
he wanted to be in the world was beyond his thinking
right now. His only concern was being the best.

The article also suggested that after you praise yourself, you create a section in your journal entitled
"Redirection." Underneath go things from that day you
wish you could do over; times when you didn't like the
result or response you got from others.

Paul surprised himself as he thought, *I think I'll call
this section "Mulligans." After all*, he thought, *Davis Love
and the Old Pro are telling me that life and golf have a lot
in common.*

So that night, Paul put "Yesterday" and the day's date
on the second page of the journal he had bought in the

hotel gift shop after dinner. He praised himself for his openness to Davis Love's comments, and for his realization that he had some things to learn about both golf and life. He also congratulated himself for taking the initiative to track down Will Dunn, talk to him, and reschedule his plans so he could stay an extra day to have his first "game of life" lesson.

As he considered the "Mulligans" section, Paul laughed. He thought about how he would have loved to replay that whole first nine. *Maybe it is true there are no accidents in life*, he thought. *If I hadn't been such a jerk during the first nine, I wouldn't have the opportunity to spend tomorrow with Will Dunn. Maybe there are reasons for things that are beyond my control.*

This was a new thought for Paul. It felt weird. Still, he looked forward to developing a relationship with the Old Pro.

As he drifted off to sleep, Paul reflected that the day had not gone as he had expected, but he sensed it was the beginning of something important. As a result, he resolved to commit any insights he had during the day to his new journal after the "Praisings" and "Redirection" sections.

6

Source of Self-Worth

*T*he next morning the receptionist at the hotel gave Paul directions to the Muni course. He headed out about eight-thirty; he wanted to hit some balls so he would be ready to go when he met the Old Pro at ten. He had never heard of a municipal course called Muni, but this added to the mystique of the Old Pro. As he approached the municipal course, he saw that it was a well-kept, well-run operation, different from some municipal courses (though it did have a public course feeling). As he drove past the driving range he noticed players in a wide variety of outfits, including dungarees and shorts that would not have passed the length test at his private club in Atlanta.

The clubhouse was an old stone building—nothing fancy. But as he drove into the parking lot, what really got his attention was the sign that said the course had been designed by Donald Ross. Paul knew enough about the history of golf to know that Donald Ross was one of the greatest golf architects of all time. He had designed hundreds of golf courses, including the famous Pinehurst No. 2, Oakland Hills, and Oak Hill. Courses with his signature on them have hosted many national championships through the years. In fact, the famous Biltmore Forest Golf Club where the Pro-Am was played the day before was also one of Ross's masterpieces. But a municipal course in Asheville, North Carolina? That seemed a little strange to Paul.

After he parked his car and got out his golf clubs, Paul bought two large buckets of balls and headed to the range. He had an hour before he was supposed to meet the Old Pro, so he figured he had plenty of time to use up both buckets. He was known to beat balls in rapid-fire succession until his hands hurt. This morning would have been no exception if he hadn't seen the Old Pro sitting in a rocker on the front porch just as he was about to buy more balls to hit.

I wonder if he travels with that rocker, Paul thought as he picked up his clubs and headed toward the clubhouse.

When the Old Pro saw Paul he smiled and said, "Put down those clubs—we are not going to get to those quite yet. Come here and sit down, son."

"I thought we were going to work on my golf game and life," said Paul.

"We are," smiled the Old Pro. "But you will find you don't always have to hit balls to learn about golf."

As Paul sat down the Old Pro turned to him and said, "Let me get right to the point, son. Why do you play golf?"

"That's a good question," said Paul. "I guess I play to have fun. By the way, you can call me Paul."

"Okay, Paul. Did you have fun yesterday?"

"Come to think of it, I didn't," said Paul.

"Why not?" asked the Old Pro.

"I was playing badly and since my performance was awful, I wasn't having any fun."

"Do you see why I asked you that question? If fun is a reason you play golf, then every golf game should be fun. I have never met a golf course or a golf game I didn't like. For me the worst a golf game can be is fabulous," said the Old Pro with a smile. "That's why I miss playing now."

"But haven't you had some bad days on the course?"

"Sure I have," said the Old Pro, "but I never thought that who I was on any given day depended on my score. I learned from bad days and laughed at bad days, but I never got down on myself because of a bad day."

"Interesting," said Paul. "I can't say that's been true for me."

"Is there any other reason you play golf?"

"I think the camaraderie and friendship is important," said Paul.

"What do you know about the three other guys you played with yesterday?"

"What do you mean?"

"Do you know anything about their lives, about their families, about their interests?"

"I don't."

"Why not?"

"I guess I was focusing too much on myself."

"Fine," said the Old Pro. "So if relationships are important to you then you have to reach out to other people, don't you?"

Paul smiled. "You're really tough, aren't you? So I said I wanted to have fun and I wanted to have some good camaraderie but I didn't have either of those yesterday. I guess I'm not walking my talk very well, am I?"

"Evidence is mounting up," said the Old Pro with a smile. "Is there any other reason you like to play golf?"

"This will probably get me in trouble too," said Paul.

"I love the beauty of a golf course. Without golf courses, most of our cities would be cement."

"Tell me about the course you played yesterday. What kind of trees dominated the landscape? What kind of birds did you see?"

"You got me again," said Paul. "I didn't notice much about anything. I was so into myself."

"What do you think got in the way of your having fun, experiencing good camaraderie, and enjoying the beauty of the surroundings?" asked the Old Pro.

"Well," said Paul, "To be honest, I was so upset about how poorly I was playing in front of Davis Love and my teammates that I was too stressed-out to enjoy myself, my playing partners, or the course."

"There is no doubt in my mind," said the Old Pro, "that you have good intentions about those parts of golf but I'm afraid you just turned golf into an achievement game."

"What's wrong with wanting to perform well and trying to be the best?"

"Before I answer that question, let me ask you another question," said the Old Pro. "What scoring system do you use to measure success in your life and when you play golf?"

"Here we go," said Paul. "I have a feeling this is probably why Davis suggested I meet with you."

"From what you told me yesterday I think you are probably right," said the Old Pro with a smile. "But seriously, where do your positive feelings about yourself come from?"

"Fortunately or unfortunately, I think they come from my performance and the opinion of others," said Paul. "If I perform well at work or I play well on the golf course and people I admire respect me and appreciate what I do, I feel good about myself."

"That's interesting," said the Old Pro. "Let me ask you a couple of follow-up questions: Is your performance always good at work and on the golf course?"

"Of course it's not," said Paul. "I have my good days and my bad days like everyone else. Yesterday was a very bad day."

"So, if like everyone else you have a bad day once in a while, or even a bad month or quarter, it's also likely that your sense of self-worth is just as regularly at risk." The Old Pro's eyes twinkled.

"That's true," replied Paul. "It's hard to feel like a winner when the scorecard says something different."

"How has that been working for you—tying your feelings about yourself to the opinions of others?" inquired the Old Pro. "Can you always count on pleasing others? Can you always rely on their support?"

"No." Paul admitted. "I learned early in life that no matter how hard I tried, I couldn't find a father figure—an adult I could count on for approval and support: not my father and not my coach. Whether it's funny or just pathetic, I guess I'm still looking. That's why I wanted to make a good impression on Davis—but my performance let me down."

"Given what you've said, don't you think you have placed your feelings of self-worth on shaky ground?" said the Old Pro.

"I guess you're right," said Paul.

IF YOUR SELF-WORTH

IS A FUNCTION OF

YOUR PERFORMANCE

PLUS

THE OPINION OF OTHERS

AND NEITHER OF THESE

ARE PREDICTABLE,

THEN YOUR SELF-WORTH

IS UP FOR GRABS

EVERYDAY

"That's a tough way to live," said the Old Pro.

"Do you have any suggestions?"

"Absolutely," said the Old Pro. "I believe if you want to be good at golf and life, you have to stop putting your self-worth up for grabs based on your performance or the opinions of others. You have to approach life and golf from the point of view that your value and self-worth is secure beyond the ups and downs of how well you might be scoring at the moment or how much applause or criticism you are hearing from the crowd. I see so many people who beat themselves up while they play golf, and I am sure that they beat themselves up when they play life. Most of us don't need anyone else criticizing us because we do enough of it on our own. So before I help anyone, I want to make sure they know that their golf game is not their score, and their life is not their performance plus the opinion of others."

"I think I see where you are going," Paul replied. "You're suggesting that if my main focus for playing golf is to win, or to impress others, it will make it impossible for me to succeed in enjoying other aspects of the game. But if I focus on having fun, getting to know my playing partners, and enjoying the beauty of the environment, I'll probably relax and play better golf."

"You've got it, Paul," said the Old Pro with a smile.

"Thanks," said Paul smiling back at the Old Pro. "You're suggesting that by using my present scoring system to measure what a good round of golf will look like, I am putting my sense of self-worth up for grabs on every shot. I'm also missing the reasons I said I have for playing the game in the first place."

"Don't I have living evidence sitting right next to me?" said the Old Pro, chuckling.

"I'm afraid you do," said Paul. "Is there any way out of this?"

"There are two ways," said the Old Pro. "The first is to play golf just to have fun, to enjoy the people you play with and the beauty around you. That's how I got my wife interested in golf."

"I never tried that," said Paul with an ironic smile, "or my marriage probably would have ended sooner."

"Not if you taught your wife that there are only three rules to playing golf," said the Old Pro. "The first is not to hurt anybody with your club or your ball. The second is not to hold anyone up—"

"That really drives me crazy!" Paul blurted.

"I agree," said the Old Pro. "That's why one of the first things I taught my wife to do was to bend down, pick up her ball, put it in her pocket, and go to the next hole. It doesn't make any sense to see anyone, man or woman, shaking over a three-foot putt for an eight or nine."

"I agree," said Paul. "What's the third rule?"

"Don't ruin the environment," said the Old Pro. "Replace your divots. Don't drive a golf cart near a green or drag a pull cart onto the green."

"I like those rules," said Paul.

"They're the best," said the Old Pro, "because if you follow them, you rented the hole. You can do anything you want. If you want to kick the ball, then kick it. If you want to throw the ball, then throw it. You rented the hole. Just don't hurt or hold anybody up or ruin the environment."

"That's wild," said Paul. "I can't see myself playing like that."

"I played that way many times when I was young," said the Old Pro. "I'll never forget playing with three corporate presidents from the Northeast. They came to Florida for a conference early in the spring when it was still cold up north. They asked if I would play with them. I said sure, but realizing that none of them had played golf since the end of October, I suggested we play a special game. Everyone was allowed one throw a hole."

"One throw a hole!" shouted Paul.

"That's exactly how they reacted," said the Old Pro.

"When I insisted, they had trouble doing it the first few holes. But then they really got into it. They had more fun deciding whether they would use their throw on the green, out of a sand trap or out of the trees. At the end of the round they said they had never had a better time."

"Wow," said Paul. "What's the second way to make sure your self-worth isn't up for grabs all the time?"

"The second way is to discover and accept the fact that your self-worth is already secure. It is not subject to how well you do or what people think of you," replied the Old Pro.

"Tell me more," said Paul.

"Let me ask you a personal question, Paul. Do you believe in God?" asked the Old Pro.

"I hope you are not going to get religious on me," said Paul. "I'm not religious at all."

"You can relax," said the Old Pro. "I'm not talking about religion. I'm talking about God. Let me repeat my question. Do you believe in God?"

"I haven't given it much thought, but I guess so."

"I hope so," said the Old Pro. "In my opinion, not believing in God makes about as much sense as saying the unabridged dictionary is a result of an explosion in a print shop."

"Okay," said Paul. "But I don't see how what I believe

or don't believe about God has any relevance to my golf game or my self-worth."

"This may be new thinking for you, Paul, but let me tell you what I have come to believe over the past fifty years." The Old Pro turned to face him. "See, the God I worship is a loving God. I don't think He made any junk, which means I think He unconditionally loves me and you. As a result, I can't perform well enough, play well enough, or do anything well enough to change the love and value God has already placed on my life—I have all the love I need. My value in God's eyes is never up for grabs.

"Now, that doesn't mean I don't make mistakes, or that I don't have areas I need to improve. But my self-worth is rock-solid in God's love. I pay attention to what I do and try to correct my mistakes every day and change my behavior, but I don't beat myself up. I know I am forgiven and accepted."

Paul shifted his weight uncomfortably. "With all due respect, that sounds great if it works for you, but I'm not ready to accept what you are saying without a lot of thought."

"Take your time," said the Old Pro. "God isn't in a hurry and neither am I. Just remember that He is only one conversation away."

"Not to change the subject too quickly," said Paul,

pausing, "but when am I going to have my first *golf lesson* and hit some balls?"

"You just had it!" said the Old Pro, his eyes again twinkling. "Think about what we have talked about and call me the next time you are down here so that we can get together again."

When Paul saw the Old Pro stand up and extend his hand, he realized the lesson was over.

As Paul drove away from the Muni his mind was working overtime. The more he thought about the short exchange he'd had with the Old Pro, the more he realized he had gotten a great lesson—one that was hard for an achievement-motivated guy like him to hear. But it was a lesson he'd needed to hear.

Later that afternoon on the flight back to Atlanta, Paul wrote in his journal:

- If my scoring system for playing golf is all about winning and the opinion of others, I will miss out on what the game is all about: having fun, building relationships, and enjoying the environment.
- My self-worth is not a product of my performance plus the opinion of others.
- There are only three rules for golf: don't hurt anyone, don't hold anyone up, and don't harm the

environment. Once you know those rules you have rented the hole.

🏌 God did not make junk. I am unconditionally loved.

🏌 I am valuable even though there are parts of my life that could be improved.

🏌 God is only one conversation away.

As Paul wrote that last line in his journal, he smiled and thought to himself, *It's good I'm not planning on giving up my day job for golf. If I were trying to make a living as a golf pro, my performance probably would be important.* Then again, the Old Pro had told him that if you evaluate yourself every day by your performance, even if you were a golf pro, you'd probably never become a great player. "You have to have a solid self-worth to endure the ups and downs of the game," he'd said.

Paul realized that even Ben Hogan, Arnold Palmer, Jack Nicklaus, and all the greats in the game had some tough times and some disappointments. In fact, Paul remembered reading about how Hogan fought his wild hook for years but stayed with it until he finally could put his game in perspective.

Looking at the clouds outside the airplane window, Paul reflected on something he once heard:

THE MULLIGAN

YOU NEVER OWN GOLF,

YOU JUST BORROW IT.

JUST WHEN YOU THINK YOU HAVE IT,

YOU DON'T.

JUST WHEN YOU THINK YOU DON'T.

YOU DO.

38

7

Back to Reality

A ll positive thinking went out the window the next morning when Paul's alarm went off. He leapt out of bed and hit the road running. He tried to eat while he was washing. He jumped into his car and was immediately on his cell phone. His three-day journey to Asheville had taken its toll: his e-mail was jammed; his voicemail was full; his in-basket was overflowing; and everyone wanted to see him.

A hectic morning was followed by a lunch meeting, a full afternoon, and then a dinner meeting. By the time he got home at nine thirty, he was so exhausted he did not even take his clothes off. He just flopped onto the bed and went instantly to sleep.

When the alarm went off the next morning, Paul was off and running again. This day looked as hectic as the last. But a quote in a magazine article on time management he was reading pulled him up short. It was by the movie star Lily Tomlin:

THE PROBLEM

WITH BEING IN A

RAT RACE

IS THAT

EVEN IF YOU

WIN THE RACE,

YOU ARE STILL A RAT.

Suddenly Paul realized his life was a rat race for results. He was addicted to making things happen and generating pay-off on the bottom line. Remembering the Old Pro's statement that life "was all about relationships," he briefly wondered what this drive for success was doing to his relationships. He already knew what it had done to his relationship with his son Jake. He hadn't seen Jake in two years. Every time they planned to get together something came up. It cut him to the quick when he last spoke to his son on the phone and his son said, "Dad, why don't you just admit that your life doesn't have time for a son? Don't call me anymore and tell me you are coming to see me. If you just show up sometime, I'll believe it."

All this made Paul think about the Old Pro. He needed to see him again more than ever. Early the next morning, Paul checked with his secretary to see if he had some free time in his schedule. Paul found himself on the short flight from Atlanta to Asheville ten days later.

8

Preparing To Play Golf

aul was excited about his second lesson with the Old Pro. As he pulled up to the Muni, there was the Old Pro sitting in the rocker on the porch of the old stone clubhouse waggling his putter (affectionately nick-named "Old Faithful"). Parking the car, Paul walked toward the Old Pro with a spring in his step.

He left his clubs in the car because he wasn't sure if he'd ever get to hit any balls. But the more Paul thought about his last visit, the less he cared.

"How are you doing, Paul?" said the Old Pro with a welcoming smile. "Are you ready for your next lesson?"

"Sure am," said Paul. "Are we going to do it here or out on the range?"

"Sit down," said the Old Pro. "Let's talk first and then I'll have a better idea of what would be most helpful. Tell me all! What's been happening with you since we last talked?"

"Well," said Paul with a sigh, "I was excited when I left here last time. You really made me look at golf and my life with a different set of glasses. But before a blink of the eye, I was back in the rat race. When the alarm went off every day, I jumped out of bed and hit the road running."

"What an unfortunate term," the Old Pro muttered to himself.

"What term?"

"Alarm clock," started the Old Pro. "Why don't they call it the opportunity clock, or the 'it's going to be a great day' clock?"

"Good point," said Paul good humouredly. "Talk about programming your mind in a negative way."

"The problem," the Old Pro began, "is that we all have two selves: an inner self that is thoughtful, reflective, and a good listener; and an outer, task-oriented self that is focused on achieving and getting things done. It's too busy to learn. And which of these two selves do you think wakes up quicker in the morning?"

"That's easy," said Paul. "It's our task-oriented self.

When we jump out of bed after shutting off the alarm our attention turns to all the things we have to do that day."

"Exactly," said the Old Pro. "As a result, few people ever wake up their inner selves. We don't even do it on vacation. We race around from one activity to another and then come home exhausted."

"What's the answer?" wondered Paul.

"The way to avoid the rat race," said the Old Pro, "is to honor your inner self by seeking quiet and solitude."

"How can you find time for solitude?" asked Paul.

"I recommend you enter your day more slowly," said the Old Pro.

Does that have anything to do with my golf game?" asked Paul.

"It sure does," said the Old Pro. "Entering your day slowly prepares you to be the best that you can be during that day. What do you do to prepare yourself to play golf? I'm always amazed at the number of golfers who have hardly any time to warm up mentally or physically before starting a round of golf. Sometimes you see them tying their shoes on the first tee. I have the feeling that you might fall into that category."

"Guilty as charged," said Paul sheepishly. "The day I played with Davis Love, I was racing there just to make our tee-off time. I got there with a few minutes to spare, ran to the practice tee to beat a few balls, and raced back to the first tee."

"I anticipated as much," nodded the Old Pro, smiling. "In an ideal world it would be best to head out to the golf-course at a leisurely pace, arriving about an hour before you are scheduled to play. Remember:

ON THE WAY OUT TO THE COURSE,

YOU NEED SOME WAY TO TRANSITION

FROM WHAT YOU HAVE BEEN DOING

TO THE TASK AT HAND—

PLAYING AND ENJOYING

A ROUND OF GOLF.

"How did you do that when you were playing a lot?" asked Paul.

"If you noticed, on your way to the Muni, you passed through beautiful, remote countryside."

"To be honest with you I didn't notice," Paul admitted. "I was thinking about a problem I have at work."

"Case closed," said the Old Pro with a smile. "Whenever I headed out here to play golf I would tune into some soothing music on my radio and begin to soak in the beauty of the surroundings. By the time I arrived at the course I was mellow and relaxed—a perfect way to set the stage for an enjoyable round of golf. I did the same thing today so I could be focused on helping you and enjoying our time together."

"It would be difficult for me to quiet my mind the way you do," said Paul. "But I can see the power in it. Suppose I developed a relaxing routine coming to the course and I arrived forty-five minutes to an hour before I was scheduled to play. What should I do when I arrive?"

"First, sit in your car, quiet yourself and think about any concerns you have that might get in your way of playing well and enjoying the great game of golf. Then lay each of those concerns down."

"Just get them out of my mind," parroted Paul.

"You got it," said the Old Pro. "Then visualize yourself

later that day, sitting with the people you played with, laughing and feeling great because you had fun, enjoyed their company, soaked in the beauty around you, and played well. Be pleased with your performance. Then head to the locker room, change your shoes, and get ready to play."

"And then I go to the range and start hitting balls?"

"Not right away—relax," said the Old Pro in a gentle, caring way.

"I'll be so relaxed I'll be like a wet noodle," said Paul with a laugh, "and I won't be able to hit the ball."

"Yes, you will," said the Old Pro. "But first, before you head out to the range, I recommend doing some stretching exercises. This gets you loosened up before hitting any balls."

"I went to a golf school once," said Paul, "and they gave me a little booklet that had the stretches they taught us. But, as you can imagine, I never get to do them because usually I only have time to hit a few balls before teeing off. If the choice is between stretching or hitting a few balls, I will smack the white pill anytime."

"Most people make the same choice," said the Old Pro. "But sometimes with a good stretching routine, you don't even have to hit any balls."

"Really?"

"Really!" he said. "In Scotland, where the game of golf originated, there are few driving ranges. So you stretch and then begin your round. I've played over there many times and it doesn't seem to hurt me or anybody else if we don't hit any balls ahead of time."

"So I shouldn't hit any practice balls?" asked Paul.

"I didn't say that," said the Old Pro. "If you do hit balls, which is by no means a bad idea, your intent should be to loosen up, not to work on swing mechanics. Right before a round is not the time to revamp your swing. You have to go with what you brought to the dance.

"Too many golfers are playing 'golf swing' on the course," continued the Old Pro, "including some of the top pros. If something goes wrong and they're hooking or slicing the ball, they try to correct it in the middle of the round. Things usually go from bad to worse."

"What do you recommend?"

"Correct the problem on the practice tee after the round or schedule a lesson with your local pro. When you are on the course, just play golf. See how few strokes you can take, regardless of whether you're hitting the ball straight, crooked or what have you. Whatever it takes for you to get the ball into the cup."

"I don't imagine people who play 'golf swing' on the course are much fun to be around," said Paul with a laugh.

"I play 'golf swing' all the time on the course. That's what destroyed my game in the Pro-Am with Love. When I work on my swing during a round all the other purposes for playing golf go out the window except focusing on my score."

"Talking about that," said the Old Pro, "while you are getting into the rhythm of the game on the range, it might be a good time to review why you play golf. Is it for fun, camaraderie, beauty, or for the competition? Make sure you don't forget about your purpose. No matter what happens on the course, you need to keep your reasons for playing golf paramount. Otherwise, as you have indicated, you may let your results determine whether you enjoy the round or not."

"I feel a bit like I'm in the third grade," said Paul. "You have made that point over and over and over again."

"That's because I want you to get it right—right—right!" said the Old Pro with a wide smile. "Why don't you get your clubs and I'll meet you by the practice green. You can hit a few chips and putts and then go to the range and slowly move from your wedge up to your driver."

"That's an interesting approach," said Paul. "I usually finish my practicing with a few chips and putts."

"Most people do," said the Old Pro. "But I think it is good to complete your loosening up routine with your driver, or whatever you hit off the tee, because that will be the first club you use on the course."

"Does that mean we are going to get on the course?" said Paul hopefully.

"Yes," said the Old Pro. "I'll ride around with you while you play nine holes."

Paul raced to the car, grabbed his clubs and met the Old Pro at the putting green. After a few putts and chips he headed to the driving range and followed the Old Pro's sequence of clubs, ending with his driver.

9

Setting Your Own Par

"Sit down on the cart," instructed the Old Pro. When Paul sat down, the Old Pro showed him the scorecard and said, "Just so you don't get the idea that I don't think your score is important, now that you're loosened up, let's look at the scorecard from the course and begin to set your own par."

"My own par?" repeated Paul.

"Yes," said the Old Pro. "It does not make sense for you to play against the course par of seventy-two unless you are a pro. As a result, I've developed a goal setting system designed to help people compete against their own par. Here's how it works:

"It starts with some brutal honesty," said the Old Pro.

THE MULLIGAN

"The par for this first nine is thirty-six, but this is a good public course and I would say that this front nine is moderately difficult. What did you say your handicap was?"

"I don't think I did," said Paul. "But I am a twelve. That's a little low, though, for how I've been playing lately."

"I've heard that before," said the Old Pro with a chuckle. "Sounds like you're negotiating a bet. Unfortunately, I won't be playing. Now, given how you are feeling after loosening up, and add to that the fact that you don't feel you have been playing as well as you should lately, and the reality that you have never played this course before, what score would you be pleased to report if we were sitting in the clubhouse having an ice-cold glass of sweet tea after nine holes?"

Paul looked over the card. "I think I'd feel good if I shot forty-four."

"In terms of the course par then, *your* par for this nine would be eight bogies and one par, but you can set up your own par any way you want."

"What do you mean?"

"Suppose you tend to start slow and finish strong," said the Old Pro. "You might want to set your par on the first hole, which is a par four, at six. Now, if you get a five on the first hole when your par was six, it is a psycholog-

54

ical lift to be able to go to the second tee one under par rather than one over."

"That could be exciting," said Paul. "So I can set par for myself on any given hole at any amount as long as my total adds up to my hoped for goal of forty-four."

"You've got it!" said the Old Pro. "Suppose you start to set eighty-nine as your goal for eighteen holes. Once you start to shoot consistently below that goal, you could lower your goal to eighty-seven and begin to stretch yourself again. With this system you are being very specific and giving yourself a goal to shoot at, not only for the entire round but also for each hole—a goal that might be more realistic than the course-designated par."

"The system sounds good to me," said Paul as he wrote down a six for the par-four first hole, a five for the rest of the par fours, a six for the two par fives and two threes for the par threes. That gave him a score of forty-four. "I think I'm ready to go," said Paul.

"Let's do it," said the Old Pro as he drove the golf cart to the first tee.

On the first hole, a par four up the hill, Paul had a good drive but his second shot landed in a sand trap. His first two sand shots caught the lip of the trap and rolled back into the bunker. His third shot from the trap finally landed on the green and he two putted for a seven. A frustrated Paul walked back to the golf cart and slammed his sand wedge into his bag. When he sat down he started to write seven on his scorecard. The Old Pro intervened.

"With this scoring system, you don't write down your actual score, only how many shots you were under or over your par, " said the Old Pro. "So write down for the first hole a plus one. That means for *your* par you had a bogey."

"So because I set my par at six, and got a seven, I have a bogey rather than a triple bogey? That's great!"

"Doesn't that make you feel better?" said the Old Pro with a laugh.

"I know what you're getting at," said Paul. "I'll just have to get that seven out of my head."

On the next hole, a long par five, Paul's par was six. Again his drive was good but his second shot landed in the rough and he had to chop it out with a wedge. His fourth shot went flying over the green and Paul shouted out, "Jesus Christ," as he slammed his club into the ground. When he regained his composure he chipped back onto the putting surface within five feet but missed the putt for another seven.

"Two thoughts on that hole," said the Old Pro with a smile. "First of all, if you're going to mention Jesus at

SETTING YOUR OWN PAR

all, I find it's always better to talk to Him before you hit your shot rather than after it. He could be more helpful then."

Paul said with a sheepish look, "What's your second thought?"

"That's another plus-one bogey," said the Old Pro with a twinkle in his eye.

"So I am two over par for the first two holes. I guess it's a lot better than being five over."

"It sure is," said the Old Pro. "Let's see how you do on the next hole, a short par four where your par is five."

Paul hit another good drive down the middle of the fairway. His eight iron hit the green and rolled ten feet from the cup. As he got back in the golf cart to drive to the green, he smiled and said, "I'm putting for an eagle three."

"You're starting to get it," said the Old Pro.

Paul missed the putt but got to write down a minus-one birdie on the scorecard. He captured his par three on the next hole and went to the fifth tee one over par. The fifth hole is a four-hundred-and-forty-yard par four. Paul hit a good drive but still had over two hundred yards uphill to the green.

"What club would you use if you were trying to hit it onto the green from here?" asked the Old Pro.

"I'd hit my three wood," said Paul.

57

"What's the probability that you could hit a three wood two hundred yards up the hill to this green?"

"Probably not very high," said Paul.

"Tell me something," said the Old Pro. "If you had a choice, would you rather be hitting a thirty-yard half wedge or a full ninety-yard wedge?"

"To be honest with you," said Paul, "I'd rather have a ninety-yard shot."

"Since the probability is not high that you can hit the green with your three wood, why risk getting into trouble in a trap or rough or having one of those difficult half wedge shots? Take out your pitching wedge and hit a shot about a hundred and ten yards down the middle to that ninety-yard range," said the Old Pro.

"If I did that with my cronies at my club," said Paul, "they would laugh at me."

"Remember what you learned last time," said the Old Pro. "Your self-worth is not a function of the opinions of others. If you would rather hit a full wedge than a half wedge, then why not play your second shot to where you could hit that kind of shot, especially since this is a par five for you?"

"There's more to this scoring system than meets the eye," said Paul.

"Absolutely!" said the Old Pro. "It's a strategy for setting realistic goals, not only for every hole and every round but also for every shot."

Paul took out his pitching wedge and hit it beautifully to where he was able to hit a full wedge to the green. Having a shot where he felt confident, Paul relaxed and hit a good shot. His ball landed five feet from the pin and this time his putt went right into the center of the cup. Paul let out a scream. "Another birdie! I'm back to even par!"

"Good going," the Old Pro shouted back.

Paul scored *his par* on the next two holes, including a beautiful three from the sand trap on the par-three seventh hole. The eighth hole was a dogleg left par five with a brook in front of the green. Paul hit two good shots, putting himself in a good position for a full wedge to the green. When his third shot landed on the green and he two-putted, Paul was thrilled to write a minus one on the card for a birdie, five on what was a par-six hole for him. He was now one under par for the round. When he got *his* par five on the tough par-four ninth hole, Paul was pleased to write down a forty-three for his score on the nine holes.

Entering Your Day Slowly

$\mathcal{S}$itting in the clubhouse sipping on an iced tea, Paul smiled and said, "Any other day if I started off with two sevens, I would have been in the tank and never rallied. Translating those scores into two plus-one bogies and not writing a seven down on the card really helped. Your scoring system, plus the suggestions for preparing to play golf, should improve my game, but what about my life?"

"As I recommended earlier, you should enter your day more slowly," smiled the Old Pro.

"Preparing for a golf game is one thing, but I'm not sure I can fit anything more into my schedule," laughed Paul.

"I know the feeling," said the Old Pro, "but it takes

discipline. Let me share what has worked for me. I must admit I don't do what I'll describe every day. It's stupid but true. It's called free will in action. My hunch is that all of us have the same problem—we know we need to spend more time in quiet reflection, but we let other things crowd that time. Maybe that is why mornings work best for me.

"When I am being really good to myself, I try to make quiet time the first priority of the day before anything else—like a phone call or time with a new friend like you—has a chance to interfere."

"So mornings are best?" asked Paul.

"I think so," said the Old Pro. "For example, research shows that morning exercisers seem to maintain a regular exercise program longer than afternoon and evening exercisers."

"Why?"

"Because things come up later in the day that interfere with good intentions," said the Old Pro. "If you take care of your inner self when you get up in the morning, the rest of the day never seems quite as hectic."

"So tell me what you do."

"When my day starts off well," began the Old Pro, "one of the first things I do is sit quietly and relax. Then I begin doing some stretching to help loosen up this old body. I mention stretching because while I am trying to wake up my body, it's a perfect time to talk to the Good Lord. He's my friend and He wants to hear from me."

"Do you pray?" asked Paul, surprised.

"Yes I do," the Old Pro asserted. "But I shy away from using that term when talking to people about my time with the Lord. When you mention prayer, people want to know how to do it. Then talking to the Good Lord becomes more about a technique than a conversation with a good friend."

"So that's what you meant when you said God was just one conversation away."

"Exactly," smiled the Old Pro. "It's so easy to think of prayer as an event or obligation rather than as a way of life. It's just simply talking to a friend along the course of your life from the start of the day to the finish."

"And, you think of God as your friend?" asked Paul.

"Absolutely!" said the Old Pro. "I think of Him as my best friend." He paused. "Do you ever talk to God?"

"No. . . . Except when I'm worried about something. I'm embarrassed to say that the only time I talk to God is when I could use His help. I would imagine if I looked at Him as a good friend the way you do, He would want to hear from me more often and not just when I am in trouble."

"That's true," said the Old Pro, "I know He is glad to hear from you anytime. The Good Book says we are to talk to our friend all the time. That's why He made us, to walk along with him. Because He loves us, it has always been His plan that we have a close relationship with Him. To prove that point, let me ask you about your son. You told me you had a son the last time we met, but we never talked much about him. How old is he?"

Feeling ashamed about the lack of contact with his son, Paul looked down and mumbled, "He's twenty-two. We don't have much contact anymore."

"Has that always been the case?" asked the Old Pro.

"Yes," Paul admitted. "I was never there for him. And since the divorce I've just been too busy. Just like my father, Jake started drinking. Then five years ago he was driving home from a party drunk and caused a serious car accident—one of his friends was critically injured. It was painful for me to see my son go through that. I wanted to help but didn't know how to reach out."

"I'll bet if he called you," said the Old Pro, "and said he was in trouble you would forget all that, listen, and still try to help."

"Despite our differences in the past, I still love him. I am sure I would," Paul said.

"God's the same way," said the Old Pro. "He's always available when you need Him no matter what you have done or how long it has been since your last conversation. But I'll have to admit:

YOUR RELATIONSHIP

WITH GOD

GETS BETTER

AND MORE INTIMATE

WHEN TALKING THINGS OVER

WITH HIM IS

YOUR FIRST RESPONSE

RATHER THAN

YOUR LAST RESORT.

"If I decided to talk with God more frequently," said Paul, "I wouldn't know what to say or do."

"Most people worry too much about that," said the Old Pro. "Now I know you said earlier that you could never count on your father. But suppose you could, and in your mind he was the greatest, most lovable father anyone could ever have. That's who your Heavenly Father is. So just talk to Him like He is your best friend."

"What do I talk to Him about?"

"Well, if you can't think of anything else—tell Him how great He is!" said the Old Pro with a smile. "Share with Him any problems or concerns you have. Even tell Him about any mistakes you've made and ask for His forgiveness. Thank Him for all that He has done for you. Then ask Him for what you need. Just start talking with Him on a regular basis and you'll figure it out."

"That sounds simple enough," said Paul.

"It is," said the Old Pro. "Let me tell you another thing I do during my quiet time. I always spend a few moments in silence, listening, in case the good Lord wants to say something to me."

"You know, I have heard people say, 'God told me,' and wondered what they were talking about. They give the impression that God speaks to them directly in a clear loud voice. I certainly have never heard God speak to me," said Paul.

"Neither have I," said the Old Pro. "Yet, I'm convinced I have heard from God. In trying to figure out how He communicates with me, I asked myself, *When do I do the best thinking? When do I think most clearly: is it in the shower? Taking a walk? Reading?* I realized that I think most clearly when I am interacting with people the Lord puts in my path. If all truth and knowledge comes from God, then I figure that's when He is talking to me. So, whenever I meet an interesting person like you, I always think to myself, *God, what do you want me to learn?* When I am quiet before Him and ask a question like that, my thoughts are directed to the things He wants me to think about. That's when it is particularly important for me to listen."

"I think most clearly when I am reading," said Paul. "Do you think that's the way God talks to me?"

"Could be. He has used both the written and spoken word to communicate with His children," said the Old Pro. "I think God talks to us all in special and unique ways. But if you are looking for a burning bush, that's already taken."

Not understanding the burning bush reference, Paul carried on: "How else does God speak to you?" he asked.

"Through His love letter to me," said the Old Pro with a smile. "It's best known as the Bible," he continued.

"I once heard someone say that the Bible stands for **B**asic **I**nstruction **B**efore **L**eaving **E**arth," said Paul. "What do you think of that?"

The Old Pro laughed out loud. "I like it!" he chuckled. "That's a humorous way to remember that the Bible contains all kinds of good advice for the art of living and messages of love from the Father to His children. Remember, reading the Bible is more than a reading assignment; it is a way to get to know and understand God and how He wants you to live in relation to Him and to other people. For example I have a plaque next to my bed with Psalm 118:24 on it. When I read, "This is the day the Lord hath made, let us rejoice and be glad in it," it starts my day off right.

"Over the years I have done a lot of inspirational reading," said Paul. "But to be honest with you, I really haven't spent much time reading the Bible. Every time I tried, I would get bogged down in some list of details that just didn't make any sense."

"You ought to try the Good Book again, Paul, if you want you to learn how to play the **G**ame **O**f **L**ife **F**irst, the way the designer of the course meant it to be played," said the Old Pro with a smile. "It's been a best seller for a long time. I seldom come away from reading the Bible without learning some important new nugget of truth about my journey."

Changing topics, Paul said, "Is there anything else you do to enter your day slowly?"

"On an ideal day, when I finish stretching, talking and listening to God, and reading his word, I do some aerobic exercise," said the Old Pro. "The Bible calls the body the temple of the Lord, and I need to be good to this old temple. So every morning I get my five iron for a walking stick and head out for a short walk with my dog. He loves it and so do I."

"What if it's raining?" asked Paul.

"I do it rain or shine," said the Old Pro with a smile. "I learned a long time ago there is no bad weather, only inappropriate clothing."

"That's a good one," Paul grinned.

"And besides," continued the Old Pro, "I found out there is a difference between interest and commitment."

"Tell me more," said Paul.

"When interested exercisers wake up in the morning and it is raining outside, they say to themselves, *I'll exercise tomorrow*. Committed people don't know about excuses, they only know about results. So if committed exercisers wake up and it is raining outside they say to themselves *I think I'll exercise inside* or *I'd better wear my rain gear.* People committed to doing something have a 'no-matter-what' philosophy."

"Interesting," mused Paul. "I'm a runner. I've entered a number of 10-K races and have been thinking about preparing for a half-marathon."

"When you make exercise part of how you enter your day slowly, you have to be careful not to treat it as another achievement game. I think it is great that you compete in some 10-Ks, but you might want to try something in the morning that helps to continue to awaken your inner self. A friend of mine was a morning jogger for more than twenty years. He is now more of a walker, but I love to be around him when people ask how far he walks every day. His reply is, 'I don't know.' They usually counter with, 'Well, how long do you walk each day?' Again my friend says, 'I don't know. My morning walk is not about getting anywhere. It's just a way I choose to enter my day.'"

"What a great approach to morning exercise," said Paul. "I can see what you're saying. The purpose of your morning exercise is to provide you with more inner peace. That's something I can sure work on."

"I end my morning time alone by sitting quietly again," said the Old Pro. "I put my hands on my knees and think about all the concerns I have about the day. As they come to mind, I just hand them off to the Lord.

"When I have laid down my last concern," continued the Old Pro, "I turn my hands upward in a receiving mode signaling I am ready to do His will as I walk through the day in the company of my *friend*. I imagine sitting here at night before I go to bed and feeling good about what we did together during the day; how I have behaved and interacted with others."

"I can understand why your routine for entering your day slowly takes discipline. There are a lot of components to it," said Paul.

"It does take discipline," said the Old Pro, "but I am positively addicted to it. When I skip a day, which I told you happens from time to time, I almost go through withdrawal symptoms, like people with negative addictions. My day doesn't go well when I have not taken time to reflect and listen to the Good Lord. I read a wonderful quote recently:

WHEN FOG SETTLES IN OVER

A SEAPORT,

SHIPS LISTEN FOR THE FOGHORN

TO KNOW WHERE THE DANGERS ARE.

THE SOUND OF THE HORN

HELPS THEM STAY ON COURSE.

WE, TOO, NEED TO LISTEN

SO THAT WE DON'T STRAY OFF

COURSE.

"I get it," said Paul. "My old habit of charging hard through life leaves little time for reflection and listening to a voice much wiser than my own."

"You've got that right," said the Old Pro.

"I can't thank you enough," Paul said.

"The real way you can thank me," said the Old Pro, "is to put some of what you've learned today into practice. Why don't we get together again in about a month?"

"You're on," said Paul. "I'll check my schedule and give you a call when I get back to the office."

Stumbling the Mumble

On the flight back to Atlanta Paul couldn't get over how much he had learned from the Old Pro. It became especially clear to him as he wrote in his journal:

> The alarm clock should be called the
> "Opportunity" or "Have-a-great-day" clock

Enter my day slowly by

- 🏁 Sitting quietly and relaxing.
- 🏁 Stretching.
- 🏁 Having a conversation with the Good Lord—
  that's what prayer is all about.

- Listening. (How does God talk to me? I'll have to think about it. Maybe when I'm reading.)
- The Good Book is a perennial best seller—check it out!
- Exercise is not an achievement game.
- End with quiet time:
  - Lay down concerns.
  - Visualize walking through my perfect day in the company of God as my Best Friend.

How about golf? On the way to the course I need a way to transition—ease into my golf game. So when I arrive:

- Quiet myself and lay down concerns.
- Visualize feeling good at the end of the round—had fun, enjoyed people, the environment, and played well.
- Stretch.
- Hit some balls to loosen up.
  - Start with putting and chipping—gradually work down to drive.
  - Focus on playing golf, not 'golf swing'—go with what I brought to the party.
- Set my own par for each hole that adds up to my hoped-for score for the day.
- Play to my own par.

Now Paul's biggest concern was whether or not he could put into practice all that he'd learned. "Only time will tell," he mumbled aloud.

When Paul got home, he successfully entered his day slowly for the first three days. But then a business crisis hit the fan and he was off and running again.

On Saturday he had a scheduled tee-off time at ten o'clock. He fully intended to get to the course by nine o'clock after taking a relaxing ride through the countryside. Once at the course he planned to loosen up with some stretching exercises, go to the putting green for a few chips and putts and then head to the driving range to hit some balls. After he was loosened up he would set his own par for the round.

At eight o'clock that morning Paul's phone rang and his plans went out the window. The call was from his son Jake, who was very upset. He had been laid off from work at a manufacturing company that he had joined after he had finally graduated from college His was still paying off his college loans and some bad credit card debts and didn't know what to do, so he was calling to see if he could come live with Paul for a while.

Paul couldn't believe it. *The Old Pro was prophetic,* he thought. He could hear him say again, '*I bet if your son called you and said he was in trouble you would listen and try to help.'* Why did I say I sure would? Paul chastised himself. *This really is inconvenient,* he thought. "Is there any other alternative?" Paul heard himself say.

"Mom is still all tied up with taking care of Nana since her stroke last year," Jake said. "So I have no place to turn."

The old last resort, thought Paul. Then, softening, he said, "When do you want to come?"

"Would tomorrow be alright?"

You have got to be kidding me! thought Paul. All of a sudden, he imagined the Old Pro standing by his side saying, *"It's okay, you can handle it. Your son needs you, so don't miss this opportunity."* With this in mind, he replied, "Let's make it work. I'll have my travel agent make an airplane reservation for you from New York to Atlanta."

After a call to his travel agent, Paul decided to keep his golf date. He arrived at the course with ten minutes to spare. *Not the best way to start a golf game,* he thought to himself with a laugh. *I guess laughter is better than tears.* Paul hit a few chip shots and putts; then tried to do some loosening up exercises. When he went to the first tee he was hardly relaxed. He hit his opening drive out of bounds. As he always did, he refused to take a mulligan when it was offered and took the prescribed one shot penalty, playing his third shot off the tee. His round went downhill from there.

In the weeks that followed, the strain of getting reconnected with his son Jake and his career problems, plus one crisis after another at work, made it difficult for Paul to walk the talk and put into practice what the Old Pro had taught him. On top of that his relationship with his girlfriend went south. The intrusion of his son into their relationship and constant references to some "Old Pro" were too much for her to take.

"I'm just hopeless," Paul said to himself. Then with a smile he said, "I didn't walk the talk—I stumbled the mumble! I could sure use some mulligans right now."

The month flew by and before Paul knew it he was on the plane again heading to Asheville. *I don't see how I can face the Old Pro*, he thought. *After all, I haven't put much of what I learned from him into practice.*

12

Mulligans Help

*A*s Paul drove up to the Muni, the Old Pro was sitting in his usual place in the rocker on the clubhouse porch. When Paul saw him, he could feel his heart pump faster. He was really happy to see the Old Pro. He had only been with him three times, but Paul felt he was a caring friend. And Paul knew all too well that he didn't have another real friend—someone he could count on, even trust.

As he thought about it, Paul realized he had been friendless for his whole life. His father had abandoned him and his coach had disappointed him. He had been deserted by the two most powerful, male role models in his life. They had both taken off, leaving him to fend for himself. Ever since, he just never had a friend. Their behavior totally destroyed his ability to trust anyone: not those who might personally draw close to him and certainly not God. He couldn't imagine God being his friend in the way the Old Pro obviously did. Paul's mind was going a mile a minute.

After Paul parked his car, he grabbed his golf clubs, just in case. As he approached, the Old Pro's warm smile welcomed Paul.

"How are you doing, son?"

Paul took a seat next to the Old Pro. "Not as well as I would like to report," he said. "This time it was not only work, but my son showed up on my doorstep."

"Really?" said the Old Pro, interested.

"Not exactly," said Paul. "He called first from New York. He just lost his job and I think he needed a friend. I couldn't believe he thought of me."

"That's great news," clapped the Old Pro. "Down deep we all need and want a friend."

"You've been reading my mind!" Paul blurted. Embarrassed by his outburst, he casually added: "Kids are hard to figure out. But losing a job can be a major blow."

Not wanting to let Paul off the hook, the Old Pro said, "Friendship is what love looks like when put into practice. It's having someone who genuinely cares about you and hangs in with you no matter what."

"I could have used a friend last week with all the turmoil my son caused in my life."

"Turmoil?"

"I just lost it when Jake moved in," said Paul. "The hassle of it all was just too much for me. To be honest, I wasn't ready to lose some of my freedom. Since Jake arrived, I've struggled at being a real father and friend to him, and I've made him feel more like a burden to me than a son."

The Old Pro said to Paul, "Have you ever thought about your father—what he was like and what could have driven him to alcohol?"

"Think about my father!" Paul recoiled. "I might have loved him when he was sober, but I hate him for what he did to my mom and me when he was drinking. No matter how many times he promised to go on the wagon, he always cracked when something tough came his way. I blame him for dying, for leaving us alone and out on a limb. I don't waste my time thinking about him!"

The Old Pro didn't say anything, he just reached over and squeezed Paul's hand.

Paul burst open. He couldn't control himself. He began to weep.

"What if your father were here right now?" asked the Old Pro, gently. "What would you want him to say to you?"

Regaining his composure, Paul thought for moment and said, "Just 'I love you' or 'I am proud of you.' When he was drinking he made me feel that if I was out of the way everyone would be happy." Paul ground his teeth. "I swore I would never forgive him. I swore I'd never ever be like him!"

"And . . ."

"And I'm acting just like my father with my own son. . . . I hate myself for it."

The Old Pro looked directly at Paul and said, "You don't have to let your past with your father or what has happened recently with your son determine the future. You see, the past can help explain the present, but it should never be an excuse for the future. You can forgive your father and yourself and have a second chance with your son.

Forgiveness is love in action. God has given you a mulligan. He will walk with you and strengthen you as you and your son learn to accept and encourage each other. Your son needs you Paul. You can turn the tide."

Paul shrugged his shoulders and then looked off into the distance.

After a pause, the Old Pro said, "Sometimes it doesn't just rain, it pours. Yet I know deep down your son really appreciates your giving him a second chance."

Eager to change the subject, Paul lightened his tone and said, "So, given the pressure at work and dealing with my son, the road to hell was paved by good intentions." He chuckled. "I needed some mulligans in my life this last month."

"Speaking of mulligans," said the Old Pro, "why don't you stretch a bit, then loosen up on the putting green and the range, and I'll meet you at the first tee in fifteen minutes. Don't worry about setting your own par. We're going to play a different kind of game today and this time you'll play all eighteen holes."

Paul took a little longer to warm up than planned. What the Old Pro had said really got to him.

FRIENDSHIP

IS WHAT

LOVE LOOKS LIKE

WHEN YOU PUT IT

INTO PRACTICE.

FORGIVENESS

IS

LOVE

IN ACTION.

When Paul finally got to the first tee, the Old Pro was waiting in the driver's seat of the golf cart. "I took a little longer to enter my round," said Paul with a smile.

"No need to apologize for that," said the Old Pro in a kind voice. "All right Paul, you're going to play eighteen holes. I'm going to watch and drive the cart. There is one new rule for this round: anytime you want to take a mulligan, take it."

"Let me hear that again," said Paul.

"You can take a mulligan on any shot you want."

"I know we've been talking about mulligans in life, but aren't mulligans in golf only allowed for the first tee?"

"Not the way we are going to play today. Not only can you take a mulligan on the first tee, you can take a mulligan on the fairway or out of the trap. If you want to take a putt or a chip over, you can do it. You can take a mulligan anytime, anywhere. Now let's see how well you do."

Paul smiled and said, "This is not my style. I don't take mulligans. But if you insist, I think I'm going to like this game."

On the first tee he smacked a good drive but it ended up in the rough. He shouted, "Mulligan!" and teed up another ball, driving it right down the middle of the fairway.

The Old Pro smiled and said, "Which one are you going to play?"

"That's easy," said Paul with a laugh, "the one in the fairway."

Paul's next shot landed in a sand trap. The Old Pro said, "Give her the old mulligan." This time Paul hit a beautiful shot right into the center of the green. "I'm pretty good, aren't I?" Paul said. "Mulligans really do help."

As they got further into the round, Paul was amazed that he started to take fewer and fewer mulligans. He was swinging with a fluidity and confidence he had never before experienced.

"How do you like playing this way?" asked the Old Pro as they drove away after another of Paul's beautiful shots.

"I love this!" said Paul. "I'm so relaxed—I'm enjoying it."

"That roving mulligan sure helps, doesn't it?"

"Sure does."

As they were driving up the eighteenth fairway, Paul turned to the Old Pro and said, "I'll have to admit this is the most fun I've ever had playing golf."

The Old Pro laughed. "Your score isn't bad, either. If you par this one, you've got a seventy-four. Have you ever shot a seventy-four in your life?"

"I've never broken eighty," Paul admitted.

"You are good."

Paul said, "I'm not good. The mulligan's good."

As they sat together in the golf cart after the round, the Old Pro helped Paul process what had just happened.

"It's amazing," Paul said. "I not only enjoyed the game and scored better, but my confidence kept on increasing. I found I wasn't thinking about mechanics. I was just letting the swing flow. I was thinking more about playing golf than playing 'golf swing.' And I certainly wasn't concerned about outcome, because I could always take the shot over if necessary. I hit more good quality shots in this round than I have hit in any round of my life."

"You sure did," said the Old Pro with a smile. "Having a mulligan to back you up, you proved you could hit all the shots. What if you could take a mulligan any time you wanted in your life?"

"How could I do that?"

"What do you do now if you make a mistake? Say you're impatient. You yell at or ignore a coworker, or you make a bad business decision. What happens?"

"I feel awful and I beat myself up," Paul admitted. "Just like I did flying over here. I was down on myself because I didn't follow through with what you had taught me."

"Would you like to know how you could avoid feeling bad when you make a mistake?"

"I sure would."

"Then let's get some lunch and talk about it," urged the Old Pro.

"Great," said Paul. "Let me change my shoes in the locker room and take a little time to write in my journal. I'll see you in the restaurant in ten minutes."

As Paul sat in the locker room, he summarized in his journal his learnings and concerns from the morning round:

> *Knowing I could receive a mulligan allowed me to perform more easily and with more confidence. The biggest thing I learned from having an ongoing mulligan is to not beat myself up for my mistakes, but to learn from them.*
>
> *As time went on, I learned from my mistakes, and so I made fewer of them. My confidence grew, my performance got better, and I began to enjoy the game. The big question for me now is how to bring this mulligan philosophy into my life?*

After Paul sat down next to the Old Pro in the lunchroom, they chatted warmly for a while. Finally the Old Pro said, "Maybe we ought to get down to business."

13

The Ultimate Mulligan

like your style," said Paul. "You know, I was thinking in the locker room about how easy it was for me to enjoy playing golf. I played better when I realized that I could always take a mulligan. I'd love to find that ease in my life. Ever since you told me, the first day we met, that life is all about relationships, I have become more aware and concerned about my relationships at work, at home, on the golf course—everywhere. I know I could use some mulligans in my life, particularly now that my son is back in the picture—and I'm still letting him down."

The Old Pro smiled. "I was hoping you would get to that place. We all can have the Ultimate Mulligan if we are open to receiving and accepting it."

"What's the Ultimate Mulligan?" asked Paul.

"It's not a what, it's a who," said the Old Pro. "It's entering into a relationship with the one who is the originator of the concept of second chances: God."

"Oh, no," said Paul. "As I told you before, I'm not big on religion."

"And neither am I," said the Old Pro, "but I'm big on God."

"What's the difference?"

"Before I get into that tell me where you are on your spiritual journey right now and where you have been?"

Paul shrugged. "Pretty simple really—I'm nowhere."

"What do you mean by that?"

"Well, when I was a kid my mom used to drag me off to Sunday school but I never got too excited about it. We went to a Presbyterian church and when I got into junior high I switched to the Methodist church, because they had a better basketball team and better-looking girls. That's what I really cared about then—basketball and good-looking girls." Paul smiled and continued, "It was at that church I met the basketball coach who let me and everyone else down when he had an affair with a teacher and left town."

"That must have hurt," said the Old Pro. "You have mentioned that coach several times."

"It did," Paul admitted. "And it damaged my faith in God and in other people."

"Why?"

"My coach friend talked to me about his faith all the time and how important it was to be loyal to God first, then your family, and then your friends. And then he goes and has an affair—breaks his wife's heart and devastates his family and friends. That's when I decided I should go it alone."

"Did anybody tell you about Jesus?"

"The coach did once in a while but then he didn't behave much like Jesus. That really bothered me. I saw all kinds of people who went to church on Sunday but seemed to forget during the week about what they had studied and learned at church."

"So you were disappointed in how followers of Jesus behaved," said the Old Pro.

"You got that right," said Paul, "so I stopped even going to church. When I went off to college, people could not have cared less about my spiritual growth. I stopped using words like God and Jesus—except on the golf course," Paul said sheepishly.

"Did you ever revisit your faith?" asked the Old Pro.

"When I met my wife Rebecca," said Paul. "She had been a churchgoer in her youth, so she thought we should get involved in a church, particularly when we had our son Jake just a year and a half after we got married. As you do early in your marriage, you try to please your wife, so I joined a local church with her. Jake was baptized there, and we would go to church once in a while, especially on Christmas and Easter."

"Did anybody tell you about Jesus?" repeated the Old Pro.

"Not really. The pastor preached about God but I never really got into Jesus."

"You got that a little backwards," said the Old Pro with a smile. "Jesus gets into you. But I'll explain that later. Did your wife help you on your journey?"

"She did at first, but then became disillusioned like me."

"What happened?" asked the Old Pro.

"The pastor of our church was fired after a real political battle. We found out firsthand that religious people can be vicious, particularly with each other. I liked him. He was my kind of guy. His faith was important to him but he didn't push it on you."

"When we saw the politics in the church and the way they treated the pastor," continued Paul, "Rebecca and I said, 'If that's what religion is all about, you can have it.' We completely turned our backs on the church. Our pastor friend who got fired tried to convince us not to do that even though he, too, had been disappointed with the way people from the church had behaved. 'Remember, churches are just full of fallible people. That's why we need a personal relationship with God,' he told us. Unfortunately, our marriage started to go south; we weren't able to hear his plea. As you said, it doesn't just rain, it pours."

"Your pastor friend was right," said the Old Pro. "That was not the time or reason to turn your back on God. Would you be interested in finding out more about knowing Him?"

"Not really," admitted Paul. "I'm more interested in finding out about mulligans in life."

"Well, God and mulligans go together because He offers the greatest mulligan of all time. After all, He forgives us for our sins—our mistakes. His mulligan works just like a mulligan on the first tee. You can't purchase one (except in charity golf events) or take one by yourself. It has to be offered to you by one of your playing partners. And, from the beginning of time, God has wanted to be our life-playing partner.

"I hear what you're saying," said Paul, "but that term 'sin' hits one of my buttons. When I talk to my religious friends, one of the things that has always bugged me is the whole concept of original sin. Why do we have to start off *bad*? Why can't we start off with original potentiality? Then we could be good or bad depending on what we do?"

"Let me ask you a question," said the Old Pro. "Do you think you are as good as God?"

"Of course not," snapped Paul. "If there is a God, that's perfection."

"Okay. Why don't we give God a score of one hundred. Then we'll give axe murderers five. Mother Teresa gets a ninety-five. Now Paul, you are struggling, but you have a good heart and are trying to get out of your own way. I'd give you a sixty-five right now. See, the striking thing about genuine faith," the Old Pro continued, "is that the Lord sent His Son down to earth to make up the difference between our score and a hundred. That's what grace and forgiveness of sins is all about. It's the Ultimate Mulligan."

"Why do we have to get a hundred?"

"Let me see if I can explain it this way," said the Old Pro. "God created us to play His course. I like to call it 'The Course Less Played.'"

"Why?"

"Even though it is beautiful, just like the Garden of Eden must have been, it can be difficult. God wants us to play His course by His rules in relationship with Him. As a result, most people don't want to play His course, thus the name."

"So we have a choice?"

"Absolutely!" said the Old Pro. "God didn't want us to be robots so He gave us free will. Just like Adam and Eve, in life we can choose to play our course or His course. When Adam and Eve chose to play the game their way on their own course, humankind was separated from God. As reported in the Old Testament, they wandered for years, playing their own course with limited success. Though God was angry about that, He still loved us and wanted us to spend eternity in His heaven. But since He is also a just God, He would only permit it if we mended our ways and became perfect—scored one hundred. That, of course, is impossible since the course is difficult and none of us can play that well, not even Ben Hogan."

"Ben Hogan?"

"Yes," said the Old Pro. "Ben was a dear friend of mine. I was greatly saddened when he died a few years ago. He was a values-driven man with intense perseverance and a great work ethic. Nobody wanted to perfect the golf swing more than Ben. Even when he was in his eighties he still practiced every day. Shortly after his death, I read an interview in the newspaper with his lovely wife Valerie. She said what motivated Ben the most was the thought of playing a perfect round. He didn't feel it was out of reach to have eighteen birdies in a row."

"Eighteen birdies in a row—that's unbelievable!" Paul shouted.

"Not any more unbelievable than saying you are a hundred on a one-to-a-hundred scale."

"You got me on that," said Paul. "By the way, I like that one-to-a-hundred concept. It is much better than calling someone a sinner. Besides, I hate labels. When you call somebody a sinner, they get defensive and uptight. But if you ask anyone where they fall on a one-to-a-hundred scale, from imperfection to perfection, nobody would say a hundred. I'm not sure that my score would be much different than the one you gave me. I'd say that I am between sixty and seventy. I'm certainly not perfect. I have a long way to go. Just ask my ex-wife, my son, or the people at work."

"Don't get down on yourself," said the Old Pro. "As I said, we all fall short of perfection, even Ben Hogan."

"I can believe that," said Paul with a laugh, "if eighteen birdies in a row was his goal."

"Well, it was," said the Old Pro. "Valerie went on to say in the interview that Ben had a recurring dream. It really was a nightmare in which he had birdied seventeen holes in a row and was standing on the eighteenth green with a four-foot putt to accomplish this perfect round, but he always missed the putt."

"That certainly would be a nightmare," said Paul.

"Unless you accept help," insisted the Old Pro.

"What kind of help?" asked Paul.

"A relationship with my friend Jesus."

"Here we go again," said Paul with a smile. "Your friend?"

"Yes," said the Old Pro. "Remember earlier I said you had it backwards when you said you didn't get into Jesus? He wants to be everyone's *friend*. He wants to get to know you."

"Really! Even me?"

"Absolutely," said the Old Pro. "A lot of people don't like the fact that the axe murderer and you get the same shot at the ball as Mother Teresa did. Yet, that's what grace is all about. It's not about deeds; it's about faith. God doesn't grade on a curve. It's a gift. If you accept Jesus as your Savior, no matter what your past has been, He rids you of your sins by making up the difference between your score and one hundred. None of us can make it to perfection without help. Not even Ben Hogan."

"I didn't know Ben Hogan was such a spiritual leader," said Paul with a chuckle.

"He wasn't," said the Old Pro. "You see, God knows that all of us—including you, me, and Ben Hogan—come short of His perfection. God requires a perfect scorecard for us to join Him in eternity. So when you turn in your scorecard, if you missed even one putt in an otherwise perfect life, as Hogan always did in his nightmare, then you will miss the cut."

"That's not fair!" stamped Paul.

"No one said it was going to be fair," said the Old Pro with a smile. "Remember, it's God's rule, not mine. The Bible says everyone will have to turn in a scorecard at the end of life. We'll be held accountable for the life we have led. People don't like to hear this, but there are no loop-holes in the Good Book about this truth. Not only must the scorecard have eighteen birdies on it for one round, but we must birdie every hole we have ever played."

"That's impossible," Paul protested.

"You're right, Paul," soothed the Old Pro. "But what if someone lived a perfect life—birdied every hole he played—and that person offers you his own signed score-card. All you have to do is attest the card and it becomes yours; you can turn it in on Judgment Day and be home free. You get to go to heaven, which, in golf terms, is like being admitted to the Royal and Ancient."

"That would be quite a deal," said Paul, "an amazing gift."

"You got that right," said the Old Pro enthusiastically. "Do you know the difference between justice, mercy, and grace?"

"Not really."

"With justice," said the Old Pro, "if you commit a

crime, you get the appropriate penalty. With mercy, if you commit a crime, you get less of a penalty than you deserve. With grace, if you commit a crime, someone else takes the penalty. The good news is that God has offered us an incredible gift by sending His Son Jesus to pay the penalty for us falling short of a hundred—not making a birdie on every hole we ever played. Because of His Son's death on the cross and resurrection, God offers us the Ultimate Mulligan in life. As the gospel tells us:

GRACE IS

NOT ABOUT YOU,

BUT ABOUT THE MULLIGAN

GOD HAS OFFERED US

THROUGH HIS SON

JESUS CHRIST.

"If I wanted to sign up to take advantage of this Ultimate Mulligan from God, how would I do it?"

"It's really pretty easy. It is the most important action you will ever take," said the Old Pro. "All you've got to do is pray something like:

Dear God,

    I know I can't make it to a hundred on my own. Thank You for sending Your Son Jesus to live a perfect life, and give me the mulligans I need to make it to a hundred. From now on I am ready to move in a new direction with Him at my side and play Your course not mine.

"Is that what they have you say in church or at a Billy Graham crusade?" Paul good naturedly teased the Old Pro.

"Not exactly," came the response, "but God will know your heart and understand your words. And when He does, you can go to the first tee. There you will find a perfect scorecard that is already signed by Jesus. Having turned your life over to Him, all you have to do is attest the card. Then Jesus will pick up your bag and you are freely able to play the course with Him at your side. But you must choose each day which course you're going to play—the old one on your own or the new one with Him."

"Will, you really know how to paint a clear picture. Thanks," said Paul. "Still, my problem is, if I sign up I'm afraid I won't follow through on my commitment."

The Old Pro took a scorecard out of his back pocket and pulled out a pencil. He wrote on the scorecard the words "commitment" and "follow through." Then he crossed them out. "God already knows you can't keep your commitment," he said. "He knows that you can't follow through. That is why you need His gift of a mulligan. Remember how you had to use a lot of mulligans in the beginning of your round when you could take a mulligan any time you wanted? You were still making mistakes. That's the way your life will be after you pray and tee it up on the first tee of His course."

"In other words, I will still goof?" wondered Paul.

"Absolutely," said the Old Pro. "But remember, as you played further into your round you didn't need as many mulligans."

"Right," said Paul. "I was relaxed and into the flow of the game."

"It will be the same with your life as you develop a stronger relationship with Jesus. His presence will make you relax and help you stay on track without needing His forgiveness—a mulligan—as often." The Old Pro turned over the scorecard and wrote on the back: "Accept and receive, because grace is a gift that you are given."

"Now I get the picture," said Paul. "I need a caddy for my game of life, just like I need a caddy for golf. Still, I bet we have to make our own tee-off time, show up and be ready to play and stick the tee in the ground."

"You've got that right," said the Old Pro. "When you show up to play God's course, Jesus is waiting on the first tee, ready to grab your bag and guide you around the course His Dad laid out—the course less played. You have to stick the tee in the ground and hit the first shot. But don't worry, Jesus will walk with you and be there for every shot you play. His course is now yours to play but *you have to play the shots.* He can't play them for you, even though He is available for support and counsel. Therefore, before each shot or decision you make, talk it over and strategize with Him."

"Wow!" said Paul, honestly impressed. "That would be like having a friend like you always by my side as my caddy."

"Absolutely," said the Old Pro.

"You certainly don't see many caddies around golf-courses today, do you?" Paul observed.

"That's true," whistled the Old Pro. "Originally golf was meant to be played as a two-man team: the player and his caddy. The caddy knew the course and he knew the player's strengths and weaknesses. He knew how far the player could hit various clubs. There were many blind shots on the links of the past. Thus, it was the responsibility of the caddy to show the player where to aim and fire. The player had to trust the caddy with his total game. They worked as a team.

"I brushed off my caddie on the first hole during the Pro-Am with Davis Love," smiled Paul.

"I would have guessed as much," said the Old Pro. "And yet the sorrowful thing about that was he just happens to be the number-one caddie at the course."

"So you are suggesting that golf is not made to be played alone, nor is life meant to be lived alone," said Paul thoughtfully.

"Absolutely," insisted the Old Pro. "The caddy worked with the player like a coach. Without that, it's no wonder the handicap for the average golfer in America has gone up rather than down over the last twenty years! Those electric golf carts have ruined the way the game was meant to be played. It saddens me to see how golfers today play all by themselves. After you get dropped off by your cart-mate you stand alone and must prepare and hit your shot without any help. You can see how far we have come away from the original, wonderful design of the game of golf."

"As well as the original design of the game of life," smiled Paul.

"I think you're catching on," smiled back the Old Pro. "Are you ready to sign up and accept and receive your teammate?"

"I hear what you're saying," said Paul. "You've made more sense than anything I've heard before about having a relationship with God. But I'm not sure I'm ready to sign up."

"I figured you weren't," said the Old Pro. "Some people say following Jesus and the instructions He gives His pupils is for sissies. But that is not the truth. The toughest test of self-esteem is bowing your head and saying, 'Dear Lord I cannot make it to a hundred without You. I can't score the perfect round.' Our ego doesn't want to admit that or give up control."

"I'm listening," said Paul.

"The first sin was not murder, adultery or any other action we call sin. The first sin was (and still is) the desire to be one's own god, to control one's own life, to stay in charge."

"I've sure seen that," said Paul.

"Don't you worry," said the Old Pro, "we'll have future lessons. The big one I want to leave you with today is that you have a chance to have the Ultimate Mulligan in your life—someone who will forgive you for your bad shots, someone who will forgive you for your mistakes, someone who will forgive you for your transgressions.

Paul looked downward with a thoughtful gaze.

"Remember forgiveness is love in action," continued the Old Pro. "God unconditionally loves you and knows you can't be perfect without a relationship with Jesus. All Jesus wants you to do is to reach out to Him in good times and in bad times. As He promises at the end of the book of Matthew He will be with us until the end of the Age. In other words, He is only a whisper away for help. See you next time. In the meantime, if you are ready to tee it up on God's course, give me a call."

"You'll be the first to know," said Paul with a smile.

The First Tee Shot

*A*s Paul flew back home, he thought hard about all the Old Pro had taught him about mulligans and a relationship with Jesus. He reread his journal notes many times:

- *We all fall short of a hundred; only God is perfect.*
- *God requires a perfect round and we all fall short of that score.*
- *He sent His Son Jesus to play the perfect round for us—eighteen birdies. Then He died on the cross for everyone, thus paying the penalty, and was resurrected. In essence, Jesus signed the card; all we have to do is attest it and we get to turn it in as our*

own perfect round—that's what grace and
forgiveness are all about.

🏌 God's Ultimate Mulligan is ours through a personal
relationship with Jesus. He gives us second chances
every day from the first tee to the last hole.

🏌 God's course is not designed for sissies. One of the
toughest tests of self-esteem is to bow your head and
admit to the Lord you can't handle everything by
yourself. You need help; you need Jesus as your
friend and caddy.

For the first time, faith in God made sense to Paul.
Still, he was not ready to bow his head, step onto the tee,
and take the Ultimate Mulligan, even after two more visits with the Old Pro.

What Paul loved about the Old Pro was that he didn't
push him. He really was a friend who was willing to walk
beside Paul, listen to him, and not judge him. By his
actions the Old Pro taught him the truth that friendship
is what love looks like when it is put into practice.

The more time Paul spent with the Old Pro, the more
he realized that Jesus wanted to be that kind of friend to
us all. *Why am I so reluctant to admit I could use help from
a friend like Jesus?* thought Paul. *I don't have to carry my
own bag or drag a cart anymore.*

Every time he met with the Old Pro, Paul learned something new. One day the Old Pro said, "I think at the end of life we are going to be given two final exam questions. The first question is, 'What did you do about Jesus?'"

"What do you mean?" asked Paul.

"Did you believe in Him—that Jesus came down to earth to shoot the perfect round for us? Do you believe that He laid down His life for us to forgive our sins and make up the difference between us and a hundred so we would not die but would live forever? It's all about faith."

"I certainly have learned from you that we can't earn our way into heaven," said Paul. "What is the second final exam question?"

"What did you do with your life? That's all about your works, bringing heaven down to earth. Again, our friend Jesus is a big help here."

"How?"

"When He said, 'I will be with you until the end of the age,' He was committing Himself to be our lifetime caddy. He is willing to lead us along the path of the course less played, and equip us to play the game better than we could have ever imagined on our own."

"That's where the mulligan comes into play, doesn't it?" said Paul.

"That's for sure," said the Old Pro.

"How many mulligans do I get?" asked Paul.

"The Good Book says seventy times seven; in other words, an unlimited number. Remember how much easier it was to play when you always knew you had a mulligan? As I've said a number of times, it's the same in life."

Every time Paul met with the Old Pro he told him more things that supported having a personal relationship with Jesus. And yet Paul still dragged his feet.

"Don't be hard on yourself," said the Old Pro on one of their visits. "Be patient. It will happen when it is meant to happen."

The Old Pro was right again. It did happen, but not for about a year. Paul was dealing with a top-management selection problem. He had always felt that he was more of a visionary leader—providing direction—than someone who wanted to or could run day-to-day operations. As a result, he searched for a president and COO to take control of day-to-day operations.

The executive he had appointed, while having great knowledge of business and many of the necessary skills, had a very different set of operational values, especially since Paul had been meeting and learning from his friend the Old Pro.

In the past, Paul had been a seagull manager. If he

delegated to one of his people, he would leave him or her alone until he or she made a mistake. Then he would fly in like a seagull, make a lot of noise, dump on this person, and fly out.

During one of their visits the Old Pro had convinced Paul that this was not a good way to manage others or his golf game. "So many people don't pat themselves on the back or praise themselves on the golf course. They just react when they make a mistake," said the Old Pro. "We treat people at work the same way. The only way they know whether they are doing a good job or not is if no one has yelled at them lately. They soon learn that no news is good news."

"How do you overcome that tendency?"

"You have to establish a set of operating values and goals," said the Old Pro. "Then wander around and see if you can catch anyone doing something right—accentuate the positive."

Finally Paul realized the nature of his past shortcomings. It amazed even the Old Pro when Paul, Mr. Type A, who always strove to be the best and achieve the most, decided to establish a set of operating values for his company with *integrity* as the number one value, followed by *relationships*, *success*, and *learning*. The Old Pro convinced Paul to rank those values because as he said, "Life is about value choices. Sometimes you can't do two values at the same time."

The executive Paul had appointed as president and COO bought into the success value and wanted to make the company mean, lean, and profitable. The integrity and relationships values carried little weight with him. Since he wasn't open to feedback, learning was not a high priority either. As a result, he was wreaking havoc with Paul's people. The new Paul did not appreciate that.

Paul teed it up with the Lord one night as he was driving to meet Jake to seek his advice, counsel, and support on this matter (yes, Jake!). Paul and his son had some rocky times at the beginning, when Jake first moved to Atlanta, but after Paul had talked with the Old Pro about having a second chance—a mulligan—with his son, he had truly reached out to him. Paul was even able to talk with Jake about his alcoholic father—the grandfather Jake had never known.

Sharing his vulnerabilities with his son began the healing process between them. Paul had grown to appreciate his son's thinking. Jake had gotten a good job with another manufacturing company in quality control. Paul thought he was a darned-good businessman for a young man! He was proud of him. He found himself more and more naturally giving Jake the counsel, love, and praise his son so longed to have. In fact, he was planning to have dinner with Jake that night.

On the way to meet Jake, Paul realized he was getting a headache from thinking so hard about the problem with the COO. Suddenly he got a blinding flash of the obvious: *why was he trying to figure this out all by himself?* As the Old Pro had said, "Help is a prayer away."

That moment Paul said to the Lord, "I can't bow my head completely now because I'm driving, but I can't figure out all this stuff by myself. My score falls short of a hundred; I am ready to play the course you have laid out for me. But I need help. I accept your son Jesus as my savior, lord, teacher, friend, caddy for life, and my bridge between You and me."

The minute he made that decision and spoke those words, Paul could feel positive energy moving through his body. When he got to the restaurant and walked in, his son looked up from the table.

"What happened to you?" he asked. "You look different."

When Paul told his son about his decision that night, Jake was happy for his father but still skeptical about pursuing his own relationship with Jesus. As a result he asked, "Dad, how will this make a difference in your life?"

Paul swallowed hard and then reached across the table and took Jake's hand. "I want to start by asking your forgiveness. I hated my father because he abandoned me and then I did the same thing to you. That is a burden on my heart that I have been living with ever since the Old Pro got my attention and made me look at my life. Can I ever make it up to you? I love you Jake and wish I had been a better father to you all these years."

With that Jake began to cry. The unimaginable was happening. Type-A Paul was holding his son's hand and they were crying together.

When they both regained their composure Jake said, "Dad, what you just did and said goes way beyond any sermon I have ever heard."

"Jake, being here with you now is exactly where I need to be," Paul said. "I know I have a long way to go, and I can't think of a better way to start this new journey than to be with you. Thanks for giving your old man a second chance—we have a lot of catching up to do." Then, getting back into his head, he said, "Somebody recently told me that the next great evangelistic movement will be demonstration. If you want somebody to be interested in the Lord, you ought to behave differently."

"I believe that," said Jake. "Talking about demonstration, what are you going to do about your top manager?"

"I'm going to talk to him tomorrow in a caring but firm way," insisted Paul. "I am convinced that with Jesus as my caddy, what needs to happen will happen."

That night when Paul got home he left a message on

the Old Pro's answering machine. "I did it!" he said. "I signed up for Jesus as my lifetime caddy. Let's talk. I still need more strategies for bringing the Ultimate Mulligan into my life on a day-to-day basis."

Before going to bed, Paul picked up his journal. He was elated to write:

> *I did it! I signed up for the Ultimate Mulligan—Jesus! But now that I am just on the first tee, how do I start to play this new course with Him as my caddy? I can't wait to talk to the Old Pro.*

When he sat down with his COO the next day, they talked frankly together. Paul told him what he liked and praised him. Then he told him what he wanted to happen differently and redirected him. In the end, the COO said, "Paul, I appreciate your honesty but I am not sure I can live up to your expectations. I am a bottom-line guy just like you used to be. I don't care whether people love me, or I them. That doesn't matter to me. I expect people to perform; I'm not here to hold their hands. Why don't we call it a photo finish between you're firing me and my quitting?" The two men laughed, and then Paul said, "That sounds fair to me, but I want you to know that I will see you are taken care of until you get another opportunity."

15

Playing the Course Less Played

*P*aul could not wait to revisit the Old Pro to personally share the new decision he had finally made to step up to the first tee. It was a whole new way of looking at life, and he was excited to hear what the Old Pro would say about how to move forward and play the new course laid out before him.

On the outbound flight, Paul reflected again on the incredible blessing that the Old Pro had been in his own life; how he had given him a whole new way to look at things and an inner strength to live life as he knew he should. He couldn't wait to get off the plane and drive over to the Muni as soon as possible.

As he pulled the car up into the parking lot he could

see the Old Pro sitting on his rocker patiently. As he approached the Old Pro his heart begin to race. The Old Pro had truly become a father he had never known and someone who he longed to be with. As soon as their eyes met, tears of joy began to well up in both of them. The Old Pro rose to his feet and embraced his young apprentice with a hug, an act which Paul would never forget. No words were needed; the hug said it all. Just like his cry with his son the night he turned his life over to the Lord, this hug was an embrace that Paul had longed for all of his life—a warm, loving and accepting embrace. It meant the world to Paul, and he did not want to let go.

At last they sat down, and the Old Pro turned and said, "Paul, I'm so glad that you made this pivotal decision to tee it up with God and seek to play His course."

"Where do we go from here with my life—and golf?" asked Paul.

"So you're still interested in golf," laughed the Old Pro. He stood up, grabbed his putter, Old Faithful, and said, "Follow me."

Paul followed him as he walked down the steps. They walked down to the left of the clubhouse past the putting green to the tenth tee. The tenth hole is a long par four which winds through a row of tall oaks and pines on either side. Playing this hole is almost like stepping into a cathedral. It is quiet and majestic.

As they stood on the tee the Old Pro picked up Old Faithful, pointed it down the fairway and said, "Paul, what do you see out there?"

Paul said, "I just see huge trees and all kinds of trouble. If I hit into those trees on the right, there will be no way to get back onto the fairway. But if I hook to the left, I'm in jail. There's no shot to the green."

The Old Pro said, "Now that's no way to look at this hole. There is a whole new way to look at this hole as well as your life."

"Really?" said Paul.

"Yes," said the Old Pro. "Did you know that the human mind and the computer have something in common? Neither the computer nor the mind know the difference between what is true and what you tell them. If you put information in a computer, it won't say 'Where did you get your information? Your figures are wrong.' You've probably heard it said about the computer 'garbage in . . .'"

". . . garbage out," Paul chimed.

"Absolutely," said the Old Pro. "The mind is the same way. If, when you woke up this morning, you looked into the mirror and said, 'You're fabulous,' your mind would not say, 'Who are you kidding? I know you much better than that.'"

"I'm sure it wouldn't," said Paul with a chuckle.

"So if the mind does not know the difference between the truth and what you tell it, would it be better to program your mind with positive thoughts or negative thoughts?"

"Positive thoughts, obviously."

"Okay then, would it be better on this hole to think about hitting a beautiful drive right down the middle of the fairway or hooking one into the woods on the left?"

"You're suggesting I shouldn't even think about the woods," said Paul, triumphant.

"Absolutely," said the Old Pro. "And don't think about results, either."

"Results?" questioned Paul. "I shouldn't think about results?"

"Maybe not," said the Old Pro with a suggestive smile. "Some of the best amateur golfers I've worked with develop a NATO attitude towards golf."

"NATO?" said Paul.

"Yes, NATO. It stands for **N**ot **A**ttached **T**o **O**utcome. That doesn't mean that these people are not interested in hitting shots or scoring well, but they are not their scores. They are not each shot. As a result they are more relaxed and able to swing freely at the ball without fear. When you are attached to outcome, you become fearful of your results. In the process you begin to program your mind with negative thoughts. You start saying things like, 'Don't hit it in the water,' or, 'Don't hit it out of bounds.' Not knowing the difference between the truth and what you tell it, the mind doesn't understand the word don't. So when you say, 'Don't hit it in the trees,' all the mind hears is: 'Hit it in the trees.' Instead, you should concentrate on where you want to go—the middle of the fairway—rather than where you do not want to go—the trees. When you are focused on something positive and have a target or goal in mind without concern for outcome, you will perform better."

"I once heard a speaker at a convention say to everyone, 'Don't think about pink elephants. No matter what you do don't think about pink elephants,'" Paul said. "Then he asked everyone, 'What are you thinking about right now?'"

"Pink elephants!" chortled the Old Pro. "That's a perfect example of what I'm talking about."

"If I start to think about the trees what should I do?"

"Back off your shot. Imagine them as friends stretching their arms out and pointing you to the fairway. They give definition to the hole."

"Interesting!"

"Once you see the golf course from this perspective,

then you can begin to build positive images in your mind instead of negative responses," said the Old Pro. "As I've suggested, the mind cannot differentiate between a negative and a positive picture. It just sees the picture and tries to direct your body toward the target."

"It's the same way in life isn't it," wondered Paul.

"Absolutely," said the Old Pro. "When you get into difficult relationships with people or circumstances you need to see them as friends not enemies. They are just God's way of helping you to focus your attention in the right direction. When Jack Nicklaus was on the top of his game he was one of the greatest generals on the golf course when it came to strategizing and focusing. Before hitting his shot, Jack would stand behind his ball and look down the fairway with his mind strategically thinking of the shot. He called this going to the movies."

"What does that mean?" asked Paul.

"He imagined himself in a movie theatre watching himself play the shot at hand and pull it off exactly the way he had envisioned it," the Old Pro replied. "Then, as he made his practice swing, he imagined himself playing that very shot. He stepped into the shot, lined up with his immediate target, and let it fly just as he had envisioned it in his mind."

"That's interesting," said Paul. "I assume he did that on every shot?"

"He sure did," said the Old Pro. "There is a story about Jack when he was playing a strategic shot in a big tournament. It was a number of years ago when they used to mike the players to catch any conversation between them and maybe hear some of the positive self talk that was going on. Jack, after going to the movies, approached the shot from behind. Just as he was beginning to pull back the club, a plane flew over his head. The distraction made him stop and under his breath you could hear him say, 'Now that was a good one.' You see, he had already played his shot in his mind. He was just going through the motions."

"So on this hole, the trees would not even be part of his picture."

"They sure wouldn't be," said the Old Pro. Then with a warm smile he continued, "Paul, this is the way you need to learn to play your shots and also live your life. In golf first focus your mind on where you want the ball to go—then the shot you want to play. As you select a club, focus on the shot you desire to play and how you are going to execute that shot. Then go to your bag and pick out the club that will get you strategically to the position that you desire. Next, always take a practice swing in the direction you want to go. That helps you put that imprint into your mind and you've got a better chance of pulling off the shot."

"That's great," said Paul. "I'd like to do that every time I play a shot from now on."

"Good idea," the Old Pro said. "Here's a simple way to remember it. We call it 'see it, feel it, trust it.' For any shot you must see it in your mind; take a practice swing to feel it with your body; and then step into the shot and trust it with your heart. It is as simple as 1-2-3."

"Let's see how that works right now," said Paul as he grabbed his driver out of the bag. He teed up his ball and stood behind it planning his shot.

"Now go to the movies," said the Old Pro. "Do you see yourself playing that shot right down the middle?"

"Absolutely," said Paul.

"Now take your practice swing and feel the shot. Nice and easy. Take time to let your muscles get in touch with what your mind is just seeing."

"Got that now," said Paul.

"Okay, Paul, now set up to the ball, get ready and freewheel it down the middle. That's when the trust comes in."

Paul nailed it right down the center.

"That's it, son!" the Old Pro exclaimed, pumping his fist: "You've got it!"

"That's easy to understand in golf, but what about life?" said Paul. "How does that concept relate?"

"It all comes down to entering your day slowly," said

the Old Pro. "As you look at your day, focus on what you want to accomplish, not on the obstacles that might be in your way. Imagine yourself sitting on your bed at night smiling because you've had a productive day. Then when the day presents itself and you see some obstacles, like trees to the right or water to the left, you can focus back on the plan that you've already contemplated. You need to see these obstacles as markers guiding you in the direction you want to go."

"I'm beginning to see it," said Paul.

"Good!" said the Old Pro. "And remember, now you have a good friend and caddy in your life, Jesus, to discuss things with along the way. That is what He wants from you: your attention and your friendship. It is that friendship that will transform your life, Paul. It is up to us to look at life as an adventure—just as we look at each hole in golf as a new adventure—and play it shot by shot, planning and executing each shot to the best of our ability with His help. We simply trust the image we have created together and let it go."

"I like that this applies to life too—not just golf," said Paul.

"That's why I love Proverbs 3:5-6 : 'Trust in the LORD with all your heart and lean not on your own understanding; in all your ways acknowledge Him, and He will make your paths straight' (NIV). Trust your caddy Jesus," encouraged the Old Pro. "Always remember, He is your friend and wants to walk with you as you play His father's difficult course—the course less played. He is ready to help you avoid focusing on obstacles and trouble spots so you can play the kind of game you were meant to play."

"Thanks," said Paul. "What we have been talking about is going to free up my golf game and my life."

Back on the plane to Atlanta, Paul found himself thanking God for the tremendous gift the Lord had given him in the person of the Old Pro. He reflected on how much he enjoyed this new life and perspective that he was experiencing. He found himself being transformed, not only by the friendship of the Old Pro, but more importantly by an inner desire to know and share more of his life with this *friend* of the Old Pro. He found himself mentally talking to Jesus as a friend, caddie, and brother. It was this inner dialogue with Jesus that changed his life. Performance no longer dictated his life. He simply delighted in being loyal to his faithful friend Jesus who was there and really cared for him.

Paul also found himself beginning to love his own son in a way he'd never known before. He began to realize that he needed to model the same type of friendship to his son as he had experienced from the Old Pro and his new Friend. He began to encourage Jake to become his own person and find success on his own terms. Paul did not want to push him the way he had pushed himself.

Jake seemed to thrive on this kind of unconditional love and support. His career began to blossom. He moved up from a quality control position in his company to Director of Production. During this process, Paul became his son's chief counselor and supporter. Indeed, the more time he spent encouraging his son, the more Paul began to understand in even greater depth the importance of the relationship with his Holy Father as the father he never had. It was scary for Paul, but he found an inner strength that could only be attributed to his new-found faith. This dramatic change came about through giving himself to his son in a transparent way, one that he had never experienced before. The more open he became with his son, risking who he was, the more respect his son gave him, and, more importantly, the closer their bond as father and son became. His life was being turned upside down. And it was not happening because he was trying to control or perform at all. He was simply *living* for the first time in his life, living a life he knew God had designed for him. His heart was filled with tremendous freedom and he could only thank the Old Pro and Davis Love III for this gift, the Ultimate Milligan.

16

The Phone Call

*P*aul kept in contact with the Old Pro over the next few years. His friend proved extremely helpful in providing Paul with strategies for bringing the Ultimate Mulligan into his life on a day-to-day basis. The Old Pro became the friend Paul never had, and, in many ways, a father too.

Every time Paul traveled to Asheville to see the Old Pro, it was a joyful occasion. They talked heart-to-heart about life, his son, his new friend Jesus, and, yes, golf. As for his golf game, he never got to a single-digit handicap, but he sure had more fun, enjoyed the fellowship more, and developed an appreciation for the beauty around him. His golf score never again had the same power over Paul that it did when he first met the Old Pro.

THE MULLIGAN

One day in the early spring, Paul felt a special urge to talk with the Old Pro. He phoned him a number of times, but got no answer. If that wasn't strange enough, his friend's answering machine wasn't on, either. Even if he didn't get the Old Pro on the phone, Paul always loved to listen to his message:

> *Life is a very special occasion. I hope you don't miss it.*
> *Sorry I have missed your call.*
> *Please leave a friendly message.*
> *May God bless you today,*
> *And remember: God loves you and so do I.*

Paul had never asked the Old Pro where he lived or obtained his address. They always communicated by telephone. Finally, after a number of attempts to call the Old Pro, Paul checked with the telephone company to see if there was something wrong with the line.

Much to his amazement the operator told him, "That has not been an active number for over five years." "That can't be," insisted Paul. "We've been talking on that line for several years." "Would you like to talk to my supervisor?" said the operator in an indifferent manner. "Absolutely," demanded Paul. He not only talked to her supervisor, but her supervisor's supervisor and her supervisor's supervisor's supervisor—all to no avail.

"Well Done, Will Dunn!"

The next day, Paul cancelled all his meetings and took the familiar short flight to Asheville. As Paul drove over to the Muni in search of the Old Pro he reflected upon the past few years and what they had meant to him not only for his own life but his family and even his golf game.

When he got to the Muni, he couldn't find the Old Pro. When he asked the starter and other staff members working around the course about the Old Pro's whereabouts, they looked at him strangely. Even when he described the Old Pro, they didn't have a clue whom Paul was talking about.

What's going on here? wondered Paul. He raced into the pro shop and asked about the Old Pro. The young assistant answered, "I don't know who you are talking about, but an old man did stop by recently and left a scorecard. He asked me to give it to a gentleman named Paul if he came by and asked about him. Is your name Paul?" Paul's heart dropped as he said yes.

When he opened the scorecard, all his questions were answered. It was a perfect round, birdies on every hole. The card was signed by Jesus and attested by Will Dunn. The Old Pro had left his scorecard with a simple note: "Paul, see you in the clubhouse my friend, at the Royal and Ancient. I got my 'Will Dunn!'"

As Paul walked out of the pro shop clutching the Old Pro's scorecard, he had two thoughts. First, he knew the Old Pro was real *at least he was to me and I know he was to Davis Love III,* he thought. Second, Paul smiled as he contemplated the possibility that the Old Pro was really an angel. The smile came from his always having thought that the Old Pro was in some ways a cross between George Burns in the movie *Oh, God!* and Clarence, the angel who saved Jimmy Stewart in *It's a Wonderful Life.*

As Paul drove away from the Muni he reflected on what the Old Pro said when they first met: *"I'd like to think that maybe at the end of my life I will hear 'Will Dunn.'"* Although Paul hadn't understood him at the time, he certainly did now. After Paul had suited up for the Lord, he remembered vividly the Old Pro's excitement when he explained to Paul about meeting Jesus at the end of his life and hearing these words, "Well done, my good and faithful servant."

Paul also thought about a verse in 2 Timothy 4:7 that he had memorized, because it reflected his old friend's life both on and off the golf course. He also enjoyed it because it was written by Paul in the New Testament: "I have fought the good fight, I have finished the race, I have kept the faith." What a wonderful tribute to the Old Pro who had given so much to Paul.

Passing the Biltmore Forest Country Club on his way to the airport, he decided to pull in and spend a few minutes at the very point where he first encountered the Old Pro (thanks to Davis Love III). As he walked onto the porch and approached the rocking chair where he first met his friend it was as though the Old Pro was still there rocking away. It brought back sweet memories of their first encounter. What an incredible journey the last few years had been because of that remarkable meeting.

Paul sat down and began rocking. He basked in the beauty of the golf course that lay before him with its towering trees and lush green fairways. Never had he appreciated the beauty and peacefulness of God's creation like this until he met the Old Pro.

Paul thought, *I can't believe one of the most embarrassing nine holes of golf I ever played turned into one of the most beneficial. The most important advice I ever received from a golf pro was from Davis Love III that day, and he didn't say a word about my swing. Plus the intrusion of my son into my life permitted me to be the father to him that my own father never was to me.*

His goal that day had been to leverage a relationship with Davis Love to further his golf game. Instead, Davis had referred him to the Old Pro—implying Paul had a bigger problem than just his golf game. What Paul received was nothing he had hoped for but everything he needed. Through their times together Paul accepted the gift of the Ultimate Mulligan that God offers everyone and the gift of a second chance in his own son's life too.

Life is full of mulligans, thought Paul with a smile. *I used to detest the word mulligan, but now it's one of the sweetest words in my vocabulary.*

Afterword

When Wally Armstrong and I first met, we immediately became soul mates and friends because we shared two things in common. First, we both love golf and have played and enjoyed the game ever since we could walk. We never met a golf game we didn't like. To us, the worst a golf game can be is fabulous. Second, we both love Jesus—not as someone trapped in a church but as our friend and Savior who wants to walk with us both on the course and off.

The Mulligan brings these two loves together in a special way.

My mission in life is to be a loving teacher and example of simple truths that help myself and others to awaken to the Presence of God in our lives. I have a simple mind that can only comprehend simple truths. When I find such a truth, I want to tell other people about it. So when Wally first told me that Jesus is the greatest mulligan of all time, you could have knocked me over. That was the most powerful, simple truth I had ever heard: we all need a few mulligans, not only on the golf course but in our lives. After all, none of us is perfect.

My mind started to soar with all kinds of thoughts about the power of a mulligan. First of all, it is not something that you deserve or can earn. Someone else has to give it to you. You can't just take a shot over in golf because you want to. The people playing with you have to say, "Why don't you take a mulligan?" Second, you have to be willing to receive it. Sometimes people's egos get in the way and they say, "Nah, forget it. I'll play it where she lies." Receiving a mulligan is not easy. And yet, if we're humble enough to accept it, we begin to realize our true potential.

Wally and I sat down together for a half day at Callaway Gardens in Georgia during the Spring of 2004, and talked into a tape recorder about writing *The Mulligan*. But when I started to write that July at my cabin on Skaneateles Lake in upstate New York, the book really wrote me. The Good Lord just flowed through me and the manuscript was finished in ten days. Since then it has been widely shared, one new friendship at a time. On any given day, someone, somewhere, is learning to play the Game Of Life First and the Course Less Played, with Jesus as their guide and companion.

I hope you have learned through this book that we have a friend in Jesus who is ready to forgive us with a mulligan and still loves us when we goof. The more we walk with Him and let His love manifest itself in us, the fewer mulligans we will need and the more we will start to live better lives, just as Paul did, because we don't want to disappoint Him or ourselves. I don't think Paul could have learned that on his own. He needed Willie Dunn.

Have you had any Old Pros in your life—wise mentors who have taken you under their wing? Norman Vincent Peale was that for me. I met him when he was eighty-six years-old when we began to work together on our book *The Power of Ethical Management* (William Morrow, 1988). He kept on nudging me toward a relationship with Jesus. He said, "Ken, the Lord has always had you on His team. You just haven't suited up yet." That became his rallying call for me to realize that God was waiting for me with the greatest mulligan of all time.

If you would like to know more about how to begin this journey, or you would like to pass *The Mulligan* on to others, or join in fellowship with like-minded folks in your area, please contact us at **www.themulligan.org**. Wherever you are on your spiritual journey, you will find some thought provoking words of wisdom from the Old Pro on our website, as well as information on how to get additional copies of the book and other Old Pro resources.

If you are interested in my book, *Lead Like Jesus: Lessons from the Greatest Leadership Role Model* or my ministry work on leadership go to **www.LeadLikeJesus.com.**

I love *The Mulligan*. I hope it will not only improve your golf game but will change your life. Thank you, Wally, for letting me walk together with you and our friend, Jesus, while we worked on this book. What a blessing!

—*Ken Blanchard*
July 2006

Acknowledgments

*T*he writing of a book goes way beyond the thinking of the authors. Mentors like the Old Pro come into our lives all the time to help guide our journey. Wally already mentioned **Duke Dupree** and **Harvey Penick** in the foreword as influential people in his life. **Davis Love, Jr.** had a significant, positive influence on both of us. And we would be remiss not to acknowledge a few other people whose thinking, cheerful support, and encouragement helped bless *The Mulligan*.

Wally Armstrong wants to acknowledge:

Jim Hiskey and **Doug Coe** for keeping my focus constantly on the simplicity of the gospel—Jesus, Jesus, Jesus.

Owen Matthews, Jack Smith, Bill Stephens, and **Ander Crenshaw** for demonstrating to me throughout the years that life is truly all about relationships.

Steve Deihm and **Dave Robie** for their coaching and friendship, freeing me up to write and teach.

Jack Keesling, Dr. Joe Miller and coach **Conrad Rehling** for being Old Pros to me and significantly impacting my life as a young golfer.

Al McDonald for his mentorship and for sharing great insights of writing wisdom.

Joe Girzone, writer of the "Joshua" series of books, for his inspiration in using parables to creatively teach about the MASTER.

Tim Philpot for his deep heart for God and for the original concept of a mulligan for golf and life.

Brent Sapp for his friendship and help in the development of the Old Pro's character.

Dr. David Cook for teaching me the mental truths of golf: "see it, feel it, trust it."

My mother **Lois** for her love and encouragement throughout the years.

Ken Blanchard wants to acknowledge:

Chuck Hogan and **Lynn Marriott** for what they taught me about the difference between playing "golf swing" and playing golf, and about how important focus is in golf and in life.

Bill Hybels for teaching me how to create a personalized journal, and helping me realize that I can't follow through or keep my commitment to God without help. I must accept and receive His grace by faith not by my deeds.

Robert S. McGee in his book *The Search for Significance*, for teaching me that our self-worth is not a function of our performance plus the opinion of others.

James Dodson in his book *Final Rounds*, for helping me realize the potential of NATO golf.

Norman Vincent Peale for what he taught me about the power of positive thinking in every part of our lives.

Jim Ballard for sharing the need for all of us to enter our day slowly.

Henry Blackaby for his insights into how God talks to us in a unique way.

Bob Buford for teaching me about the final exam and that Jesus makes up the difference between us and a hundred. What a wonderful way to teach about grace.

Bob Toski, my coauthor for the *Golf Digest* article "The One Minute Golfer," as well as **Tom Wischmeyer, John Darling, Dave Emerick,** and all the great teachers from the Golf University, for all they taught me about the wonderful game of golf.

Keith Jackson, the great NFL tight end, for sharing with me that BIBLE can stand for **B**asic **I**nstruction **B**efore **L**eaving **E**arth.

Art Turock for teaching me the difference between interest and commitment.

Michael O'Connor for teaching me about how important it is for organizations to have rank-ordered values.

Tony Robbins for teaching me what the brain and the computer have in common.

John Ortberg for sharing with me how absurd the term "alarm clock" is.

Wally and *Ken* want to acknowledge:

David Moberg, Senior Vice President and Publisher of W Publishing Group, for believing in us and in *The Mulligan*, and for helping make things happen; **Thom Chittom,** our managing editor, for his patience and dedication to produce the best possible manuscript; **Lori Lynch,** for all her wonderful book and graphic design work, and for her continual effort to make sure all of our changes made it into the finished pages; and **Chris Tobias** for his creative cover, and for his flexibility in listening to and integrating our suggestions.

ACKNOWLEDGMENTS

Bob Jewell for catching our vision for *The Mulligan* and being willing to organize and implement a strategy to make it happen through Old Pro Resources.

Phil Hodges for all his encouragement, feedback, and help throughout the writing of this book.

Phyllis Hendry and all the Lead Like Jesus staff for praying for us and cheering us on.

Kevin Small for his feedback on the book, work on the contract, and all his creative marketing thinking.

Richard Andrews for all his help on our contract and for making this book a reality.

Nancy Jordan for putting our ramblings down on paper in a loving, caring, and encouraging way.

Anna Espino, Dotie Hamilt, Martha Lawrence, and all the great people at the Ken Blanchard Companies who have been so patient and helpful to us throughout this project.

Debbie Armstrong and **Margie Blanchard,** our wives, for their love, patience, and inspiration to press on with *The Mulligan*.

And finally, last but not least, to **Jesus** for making it all possible. To You be all honor and glory. Amen.